MW01268497

WAGES SO LOW YOU'LL FREAK

Mike Pudd'nhead
P.O. Box 7458
Mpls, MN 55407

mikepuddnhead@gmail.com

rabbledistro.com

ISBN 9780615799483

Printed by
Black Cat Press
4508 118 Avenue
Edmonton, Alberta
Canada T5W 1A9
www.blackcatpress.ca

Table of Contents

2010

The Election

3

Why Happiness?
by 23-year-old Mike Pudd'nhead
2008

A few minutes before bar close the other night my friend said he was glad to hang out, that for a while there he hadn't seen much of me. I said yeah, I just went through a period where I wasn't going out too often. He said he'd been there. And then I said, happiness will do that to you. Keep you shut in like some sort of lunatic. But I've learned my lesson. Never again with the happiness.

That's why I'll be spending this Valentine's Day alone. Happiness — and I'm talking about the lovey-dovey kind with the smooching and the orgasms — requires a certain level of commitment. An investment, say, of time, feelings, and breakfasts. Well I have lots of writing and radical organizing to do, and I really don't have time to cook breakfast.

*

When I was in college I took a Russian History class and I remember Professor Stavrou[1] telling me this anecdote about Lenin. I don't remember the exact details - I spent my last year in college blacked out on vodka and vomiting in buckets - but I can paraphrase.

The story was that Lenin and this scorching hot Bolshevik girl had climbed to the top of some mountain peak and were enjoying a picturesque Russian afternoon together. The sexy bolshy girl was talking about the landscape's natural beauty and making rising sun metaphors and other suggestive banter. But all Lenin could talk about was those damn Mensheviks[2].

---

[1] You may know him from the sandwich named after him at Victor's, a competitor of my current employer

[2] Competing Communist contemporaries of Lenin's who are now only a footnote in Russian history

4

Now granted Lenin obviously got a couple things wrong. But I think it's fair to say that in the history of workaholics, this fellow stands out as a guy who accomplished quite a lot. And Lenin didn't give a damn about smart sexy ladies.

*

I mentioned my drinking earlier and I feel I ought to clarify a couple points.

I only drink because I'm interested in revolutionary union organizing. Organizing in my experience is all about looking good and acting cool. Nobody wants to risk their job on the ideas of a bespectacled loser. And regardless of what television would have you believe, only losers drink O'Doul's.

Also asking somebody to join an organizing drive is kind of like asking somebody on a date, and usually your chances improve if they're really trashed.

All by way of saying that my being alone on Valentine's Day really has nothing to do with my "alcoholism."

*

Another Russian historical figure with famous facial hair who shared Lenin's take on relationships was Tolstoy. Tolstoy was a party boy in his younger years, but as he aged and became more of a rock star literary dude, he started thinking – I bet I could start my own religion. So he did.

A big part of Tolstoy's religion was the idea that no one should have sex ever. He explains this position clearly in the epilogue to the *Kreutzer Sonata*[3]. You can also see his anti-

---

[3] On original sin and why we can do better:

"This would, in reality, be the same as though a farmer should not consider as a sowing that sowing which gave him no crop, but, sowing in a second and third place, should regard as real sowing that which was successful."

Makes perfect sense to me...

5

sex trend in the popular *Anna Karenina*. Levin, the main male character, is mostly interested in crops and God. He ends up with a bumping farm and does not die in the novel. Anna is mostly interested in love and doing it. She ends up throwing herself under a train. Case closed.

Tolstoy saw chastity as an ideal, and he thought we should always strive to be perfect. I'm kind of a perfectionist myself — I walk several miles a day[4], I eat lots of vegetables[5], I smile often and try to make a good first impression[6] — and that's basically why I never have sex.

*

When you're talking to your coworkers about forming a union, the first step is to get them agitated. You have to ask a bunch of questions until you figure out what it is about their job that they hate the most. So for instance:

How long have you worked here? Do you always work the night shifts? Your hours change week to week? How much notice do you have for your schedule? Doesn't that make it hard to have a life outside of work? Have you ever had to back out on commitments because you got scheduled to work?

Thing is, folks will generally agree that the bosses don't pay enough, that the managers can be dicks, that paid sick days would be radical, etc. But unless they're really pissed off, they're not going to pick a fight with management about it.

That formula translates to all aspects of life. Maybe you dislike your Shakespeare teacher. He's pompous and calls his students inane and insular. But you'll probably sit passively and suffer through class unless:

---

[4] To and from my car, mostly
[5] #6 — Vegetarian Sub — lettuce, sprouts, tomatoes, cucumbers, and avocado spread.
[6] Three $2 tips = one 6-pack of tallboys

A. He threatens to fail you
B. He starts making passes at that cute girl with the pink-streaked hair who you've been meaning to talk to but the situation hasn't manifested yet.

In the case of A, maybe you send an e-mail to the Dean of the Liberal Arts College. In the case of B, maybe you work up the courage to talk to your classmates[7] and organize a standing-on-your-desks "Oh Captain My Captain" moment where you put that bastard in his place.

People don't pick fights unless they're agitated. And this world contains several fights worth picking, what with the capitalism, patriarchy, racism, homophobia, and so on. If we're serious about combating oppression, we can't risk finding happiness.

It's like in Red Dawn when the downed American pilot tells Charlie Sheen that "all that hate's gonna burn you up inside, kid." And then Charlie Sheen says, "It's what keeps me warm."

*

Do you know what Adolf Hitler did the day before he died? He married Eva Braun. They had been in a loving relationship for sixteen years but could never marry because of Hitler's celebrity. With the Red Army closing in they were like, what the hell, let's go crazy!

Hitler is also famous for being a fascist mass-murdering maniac. Further evidence that love does strange things to the mind.

*

Before I got serious about union organizing, I had a couple decent relationships myself. I remember limiting my

---

[7] But not that girl with the pink-streaked hair. She's probably sleeping with the professor by now.

7

drinking to a day or two a week, working on a novel, having sex, etc. It horrifies to me think of it now, but for a while I was even looking into grad schools!

Academia is a wasteland of hypocritical pretty boys. You can write papers about revolutionary labor unions all you want, but you can't do any union organizing sitting behind a desk grading essays. Thankfully I wised up and got a real job.

*

This Valentine's Day falls on a Thursday, and I'll be working all night. I'll probably be good and agitated, so I'll drink beers in the basement with my coworkers and talk about our bullshit jobs. I'll toss out a lot of what if's – what if we went downtown to the franchise office and demanded a raise, what if we had a casual dress day and all left our stupid uniforms at home, what if we all told the manager we were closing early tonight so we could go to the bar.

By now I've become better at agitating than at flirting anyway, so Valentine's Day falling on a Thursday works out pretty well. I'll have a good night of slurred conversations, give my coworker a ride home, and probably wander back to the house around 6am.

At home I'll make some food out of a box, brush my teeth, check my e-mail/Myspace, and then pass out cold. I imagine I'll be drunk enough that I won't remember my dreams. Which is handy, because in truth I sometimes dream about sex and it's awful tempting. But I'm above that now.

*

So cheers to all the agitators out there rocking the celibate life. Don't get too down on yourself this Valentine's Day, and if you do then turn it into something positive by agitating about something totally unrelated, like your job.

Oh, and to all the popular guys who drink responsibly with their smart sexy girlfriends – happy fucking Valentine's Day, Hitler.

8

Introduction

This is the story of a union campaign that consumed my life for the years 2007-2010. The idea was that we'd organize a union at a Jimmy John's franchise in Minneapolis. What would that look like? We had no clue. Now I do and I will tell you all about it.

I wanted to make this story about the wonderful people I met and worked with during the course of this union campaign. Problem was there were too many of them. You'll never keep them all straight. Don't try.

The only way I knew how to write this story was to make it about me and my experiences. So allow me to introduce myself. Or rather, allow me to introduce my 22-year-old self.

Back in April 2007 I was a punk living in a house with a bunch of other punks in South Minneapolis. I had been bouncing between basement shows for a few years and had reached two conclusions about the world and punk rock.

Conclusion 1: As technology advances, people should have to work less. For instance, if 10 people can grow the same amount of corn in a year that used to take 100 people, we all should be working less. Instead we have to find useless jobs like advertising and cashiering. That made me bitter.

Conclusion 2: Trainhoppers are rich kids. It seemed that all these primitivist old thymey hobos had a posh parent's house in some suburb to run back to when times got tough. The punks who didn't grow up wealthy typically had been working since they were old enough to push a mop. They were never the cool kids in the punk scene and they usually worked at Jimmy John's.

Based off of those two conclusions, I took the only logical course available. I got a job at Jimmy John's and embarked upon a quest to organize America's first fast food union. This is the story of that quest. Enjoy!

2007

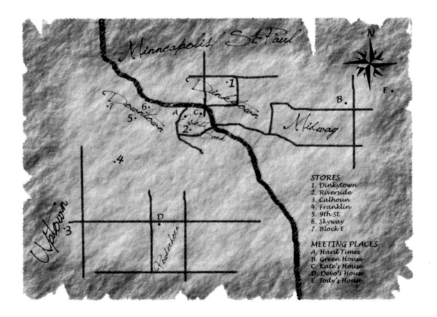

STORES
1. Dinkytown
2. Riverside
3. Calhoun
4. Franklin
5. 9th St.
6. Skyway
7. Block E

MEETING PLACES
A. Hard Times
B. Green House
C. Kate's House
D. Devo's House
E. Jody's House

8

Thanks Max for the maps!

April 21ˢᵗ, 2007

I've been working at the Dinkytown Jimmy John's since February. I started off working 10 hours a week, but this week I was scheduled 28. I'll be lucky to get 25 - we don't have guaranteed hours.

Chapter 1
My First 1-on-1

The first time I ever approached one of my coworkers at Jimmy John's about forming a union was after a Spaghetti Dinner at my house. My upstairs roommate had been hosting a series of Frankenstein-themed Spaghetti Dinners. We had Bride of Spaghetti Dinner, Son of Bride of Spaghetti Dinner, Stepchild of Son-In-Law of Bride of Spaghetti Dinner, and so on. This was one of those.

A few days earlier I had been working a shift at Jimmy John's Gourmet Subs[9] when I ran into an old friend of mine. Kate was an outgoing Indian woman I had met a couple punk houses back in my rental history. She shared a hometown and maiden name with my grandma but was nowhere near as racist or old.

Kate and I made sandwiches together on a simple cold table sandwich line. She did most of the work, as I had no idea what I was doing. I'd only been working at Jimmy John's a month and hadn't learned much in the way of food preparation. I was coming from the world of pizza delivery and still upset that absent any deliveries I couldn't sit and read sci-fi books. Kate in contrast excelled at her job and worked freaky fast[10].

Kate was covering a shift at the Dinkytown JJ location but also worked 6 days a week at the Riverside location. She told me that between the two stores she was working 7 days a week with doubles on two of the days, for a grand total of 50

---

[9] Hereafter referred to as Jimmy John's, JJs, or the place where dreams go to die
[10] A JJs corporate catchphrase

11

hours a week at $6.75 an hour, 60 cents above the minimum wage at that time.

Kate had recently graduated from the University of Minnesota with a librarian's degree but had been unable to find work in that field. So she'd returned to campus to serve up the fastest most generic sandwiches in fast food.

I tried to convince her that the weekend had long been an established standard in American working life, but her outstanding debts argued otherwise. Ultimately I invited her to our Spaghetti Dinner where I planned on approaching her about organizing a union for Jimmy John's workers.

I had been a member of the Industrial Workers of the World[11] for about a year and in that time had attended two IWW Organizer Trainings. During those trainings, attractive young organizers pounded into my head that the basic unit of union organizing was the 1-on-1 conversation. The first step was setting up the 1-on-1, which proved more challenging than it sounded.

The goal was to set up a time and place outside of work to discuss work issues. You weren't supposed to talk too much about it at work, partly because you didn't want management to find out and partly because workers speak differently about work when they're on the clock. The trick was to keep the conversation short and set up a time and location where you could have a sober 1-on-1 discussion about work.

Rather than follow those guidelines, I spent my entire shift grilling Kate about her working conditions. I wanted to ask her if she would meet up somewhere later to discuss our problems at work, but I didn't know how to do it. So instead I invited her to a party at my house. Rather than choosing a setting where Kate would feel comfortable and we could have an intimate conversation, I had picked a party where I would feel comfortable and could get shitty drunk.

---

[11] Hereafter referred to as the IWW, the Wobblies, or the world's best-dressed labor union

All by way of saying I was brand new to union organizing and pretty much making it up as I went.

At the Spaghetti Dinner I could not find the right time to mention the union to Kate. I wanted to talk to her when she was alone so she wouldn't be distracted. Problem was I had invited her to a party. When are you alone at a party?

At the end of the night we were standing around a bonfire in the backyard and Kate said she was on her last cigarette before leaving. I was determined to bring up the union and this seemed like my last chance so I blurted it out:

"Remember when we were talking about how you work 7 days a week and get paid shit?"

"Yeah, why?"

"Well how would you feel about organizing a union at Jimmy John's?"

Kate went on to tell me that someone in her family was a big unionist and she'd always been a social justice advocate and hell yeah she wanted to help organize a union at Jimmy John's! Success!

From that moment I was hooked. And thus began 4 years of my life as a union organizer at Jimmy John's.

Chapter 2
The First Meetings

April 21st, 2007

Wil has been working at the Calhoun store since around October 2006. We had been discussing organizing at JJs since Wil got the job. We are focused on the franchise we work in, which has six stores and is opening a seventh next weekend.

Wil was a tall skinny 20-year-old with a head for radical history and a horror for post-secondary education. A couple years earlier I had interviewed Wil about his band Friendly for a zine. During that interview he mentioned to me that a new IWW branch was starting up in Minneapolis, and several months later he invited me to my first IWW meeting. Since then he'd

13

joined the IWW, started delivering for JJs at the Calhoun Square location in Uptown, and become my best friend.

When I told Wil about my 1-on-1 with Kate he got fired up and immediately began writing down a list of people to approach about unionizing.

Wil had a bunch of childhood friends that worked at the Dinkytown store with me. They were all 17-20 year-old St. Paul kids. Their interests included graffiti, bicycles, noise bands, hip hop, and smoking weed.

Over the course of a couple weeks Wil contacted all of them and spoke with them about forming a union. Our first meeting was scheduled to be at Powderhorn Park after the Mayday parade[12].

On Mayday parade day I hung out with Wil and saw Kate and a few of the Dinkytown JJ guys, but we never convened a meeting. I spent the day drinking beer-cozied cans of Black Label and kicking around a soccer ball. Later I went to a basement show and drank Black Label sans cozy. It was all somewhat discouraging.

My coworkers Aaron, Adam, and Uriah lived at a house in Midway St. Paul called the Green House. Wil and I decided we'd have our second first union meeting there, and then they would have to attend.

The meeting started half an hour late. In attendance were myself, Wil, Aaron, and 3 random guys who didn't work at Jimmy John's. We sat on couches in the Green House's barren yet filthy living room, sipping on cheep beers.

Aaron, whom Wil had described to me in great philosophical detail as his longstanding nemesis[13], was a shitty coworker. Unreliable, irresponsible, loud and obnoxious. Not my first choice for our organizing committee.

---

[12] A May 1st tradition in South Minneapolis. It's a hippie holiday and it's international workers day. So it's pretty much the ultimate red-green alliance parade.

[13] Not his enemy, but his opposite, or something like that. His explanation was better.

14

The meeting began with no facilitator and no agenda. Aaron dominated the conversation. He would alternately go on a long-winded rant about the corporate bullshit he had to put up with and then follow that up with an argument about how the job was actually pretty rad because he got to ride his bike and could get away with anything[14].

After a while Uriah and Adam showed up and we managed to steer the conversation in a more productive direction. Uriah was concerned about our assistant manager's forthcoming promotion and thought that our jobs were in jeopardy. We decided to write a letter to our district manager about our concerns, which we would have everybody at the Dinkytown store sign before submitting. I was pumped and thought that our second first meeting had been a great success.

In retrospect:

What We Did Do At The Meeting:
- Drink beer
- Start late
- Slightly outnumber the non-JJ workers in attendance
- Decide to write a letter without tasking anyone to write it or collect signatures

What We Did Not Do At The Meeting:
- Choose a chair/facilitator
- Take notes
- Follow an agenda
- Accomplish a whole hell of a lot

Still, it was a start.

---

[14] He got fired two weeks later

Chapter 3
Commitments

June 4th, 2007
I'm fucking really overwhelmed with all the stuff I'm trying to do lately. The JJ campaign is my #1 priority, and then the zine I'm working on, then the band I'm trying to get going with Eric, then the IWW branch stuff, then Jack Pine and Welcoming Committee meetings, and then somehow I have to find time to make out with girls and hang out with friends and shit. Oh well, at least I'm busy.

The summer of 2007 found me busier than I'd been in years. I was working long weekend night shifts at Jimmy John's as well as a couple day shifts. I was volunteering at Arise Bookstore[15] and getting more involved at the Jack Pine Community Center[16]. I had joined the RNC Welcoming Committee[17] and was active on one of its subcommittees. After not playing music for over a year I had started practicing in a band we would eventually call *Terracide*[18].

The previous winter I had broken up with my girlfriend and gone crazy and left town on a tour of the United States with my dog. Soon after I got back my ex reunited with her ex who was my ex-best-friend and it was all very upsetting. I of course had to write a zine about it, and I was busy with that too.

The JJ union committee had decided against the Green House as a permanent meeting space and had moved our meetings to Kate's house on the West Bank. I was talking to almost all my coworkers about working conditions and inviting

---

[15] Collectively-run Minneapolis anarchist bookstore at 25th and Lyndale
[16] Collectively-run Minneapolis anarchist community center at 30th and E. Lake
[17] Collective formed around protesting the 2008 Republican National Convention in St. Paul
[18] Collective formed around sci-fi metal horror punk fantasy thrash and democratic procedure

them to our meetings, but the only one who seemed serious and was coming to meetings was a guy named Jody.

Jody was a St. Paul native with a swanky bike, a soft voice, and occasionally a moustache. He did not appreciate being scheduled shifts only a day in advance and working different hours every week. He immediately contributed creative ideas to our committee, like making a blog for covering shifts and organizing a JJs-themed bike race to bring together workers from different stores.

It was around this time that I picked up a habit of making lists of people to call. When I could find the time I'd brainstorm names. 5 people to invite to the meeting, 3 people about Jack Pine junk, 2 people about band practice, 2 people about the Welcoming Committee, 2 people about some other damn thing. I'd spend an hour making 15 phone calls then run off to work on some other project.

Union organizing is consuming work, and intuitively you would think that when you're heavily involved in an organizing campaign you have no time for any other projects. In my experience though, I could juggle all kinds of other commitments alongside the JJ campaign, so long as the campaign was inspiring for me. And early on it was nothing but inspiring.

The IWW preaches an ideology of "Solidarity Unionism" that emphasizes collective direct action over legal representation and bargaining. So in my mind we would agitate around these smaller store issues, organize small actions to empower workers and win concrete gains, then as we grew our committee through actions we'd begin organizing around larger issues and eventually stage work stoppages and win an across the board raise that would inspire millions of workers in fast food to organize and take control of their workplaces. Piece of cake.

Chapter 4
Kate's Firing

June 10th, 2007

Kate got fired on Thursday. She had gone to the clinic Wednesday, been diagnosed with strep throat, and received a penicillin shot. Thursday morning she tried going into work, but her cousin stopped her. She called Riverside general manager David and told him she couldn't come in. He said "okay." An hour later David called her and fired her.

The sick policy at Jimmy John's, like most restaurants, was that if you were sick you called and told your manager. The manager would then decide if they needed you. If so, you came in and worked anyway. Alternatively, you could look for your own replacement. If you called in sick too many times they would fire you, even if you brought a doctor's note explaining your contagious sickness. This is how my friend and fellow union member Kate Sinna got fired.

She called me Thursday night and told me about her bullshit firing. She was spitting mad but not sure she wanted her job back. A recurring difficulty in organizing is that once you get people to discuss their problems at work, they realize how shitty their job actually is and are less enthusiastic about scrubbing floors and upselling bacon.

To me this felt like make or break time for the campaign. Kate was 1 of only 4 solid committee members we had, and the other 3 of us were all straight white dudes. Probably I was tokenizing, but we'd been discussing in our committee meetings that if we were going to succeed in our organizing we needed to grow our committee to be more representative of the workforce, which was majority white and male but also included quite a few women and people of color. I felt we couldn't abide Kate's firing.

Friday afternoon I went over to Kate's house and had a long talk with her. She was on the verge of going out of town for the weekend, but I convinced her that fighting for her reinstatement would be an empowering experience for

18

everyone involved and she'd feel a lot better confronting them about it.

That Sunday we met on Kate's front porch, which was kinda cramped for 11 people. Only 6 of us worked at Jimmy John's. Notably present was Joe Blackseer, my 18-year-old coworker at Dinkytown who had never attended one of our meetings. Joe was a dreadlocked hip hop artist from the rough side of St. Paul.

The other 5 people at the meeting were roommates and a couple local wobblies. I'd invited non-JJ workers to the meeting specifically because I felt this was an important meeting and I wanted to create a shoulder-to-shoulder setting[19].

I de facto facilitated and we stayed on point with everybody participating. We decided that the next morning we were going to have people call Riverside JJs during their lunch rush and ask to speak to GM David about Kate's firing.

We figured that with all the phones constantly ringing during their busiest time we could fuck up their lunch rush deliveries and make the store absolute chaos. While that was going on, Kate would bring a letter we'd written about her firing to the Dinkytown store and collect signatures. Then at 1pm Wil, Kate, Jody, Joe Blackseer, and myself were going to walk into the store and confront David about her firing. At which point he would either relent and rehire her or we'd all get our asses fired.

Chapter 5
Our First Job Action

It's early in the afternoon on a hot summer day. Wil, Kate, Jody, Joe, and myself are walking down the sidewalk from Kate's house towards the Riverside Jimmy John's. We're all wearing our JJ work shirts. We figure we will be more impressive when we confront Kate's GM David if we're all

---

[19] Cramped is good for organizing committee meetings. Avoid large open spaces.

wearing the same shirt. We also want it to be obvious that we're JJ workers — besides Kate, none of us work at the Riverside store.

I barely slept last night. I was thinking that this action wouldn't work if we couldn't get at least four people to participate in the march on the boss. At the meeting five of us had said we were down, but what if somebody flaked? This morning I was a ball of nerves as Wil and I rode our bikes to Kate's house. Jody and Kate were already hanging out on her porch when we arrived. Joe wasn't far behind.

As we walk we speculate on the atmosphere in the Riverside store. Hopefully the workers aren't too stressed. Before the phone zap began we called in a delivery and passed the driver $80 from the IWW to disperse amongst his coworkers. Kate and I had talked to him about it at the bar the night before. The idea was we would compensate drivers for lost tips due to the jammed phone lines, and we'd give inshoppers some money too for the extra hassle of answering phones and dealing with a freaked out manager. The driver was all smiles and told us to "fuck them up."

The phone zap seems to have gone just as we planned. We didn't make it public, but we put a call out on IWW list-serves and sent mass texts to our friends asking them to call the Riverside store between 11:30 and 1. They were supposed to ask for a manager and then say something like, "You shouldn't have fired Kate for having strep throat, please rehire her." All the phones would be ringing constantly during the busiest time of the workday, and the manager would be hearing over and over again how he'd done something wrong. Plus somebody would have to answer the phones, so they'd be short-staffed and the customer lines would seem endless.

When we arrive at the store, Kate's the first one through the door. There's no sign of David but all the workers regard us with half-smiles and raised eyebrows. The driver we gave the $80 tip walks past me grinning from ear to ear and tells me it was *cur-ay-zee* at work today. Kate's talking to an inshop woman who says she'll go get David out of the back office.

20

He comes out into the kitchen and he's talking a mile a minute. You ruined my lunch rush! This isn't about Kate it's about hurting our sales! I've been working 10 hours! We couldn't get deliveries made! What do you think you're doing getting everyone to call the store! And so on. None of it really connects into a logical argument.

We ask him to calm down and get him to come out into the dining area, where we surround him. We explain to him that we made Myspace[20] posts asking people to call the store because we thought Kate was fired unfairly. She is a hard worker and she needs her job. She has a doctor's note proving that she has strep throat. He needs to rehire her.

David tells us that he can't rehire her, because his boss Brian the district manager was the one who told him to fire her. This is unexpected. David says that after Kate called in sick he talked to Brian, who decided that she'd been missing too much work lately. Corporate and upper management like to say that "it's easier to get a new dog than to teach an old dog new tricks." Meaning we are dogs and if we develop bad habits, like getting strep throat twice in a month, it's easier to just fire us.

We're full of adrenaline and not ready to back down, so we tell David that if Brian was behind her firing then we need to talk to Brian. David leaves to make a phone call, then returns and tells us that Brian and the owner's son Rob are both on their way to the store. We can wait at a table in the dining area.

As soon as we sit down the energy starts to drain out of us. The theory behind a march on the boss is that you have strength in numbers. We had David 5 to 1. Round two with the bigger bosses we haven't even planned on confronting will be 5 to 3. That's not so good a ratio considering all 3 of them have the authority to fire us. Probably we're waiting to be fired.

Nobody's talking, so in a flash of inspiration I suggest that we play 20 Questions while we wait. The way 20 Questions works is somebody picks a thing – any thing – and the rest of

---

[20] Facebook before Facebook

us ask yes/no questions until we guess the thing. It's a great game to play in a tour van, because it doesn't require any materials, only imagination.

Wil has picked a thing. Is it a person? Yes. Do I know her? No. If she was at a show would she dance? Depends on the show probably. Does she advocate the peak oil theory? I doubt it. Would you?

It works and before long we're chatty and smiling. Kate's inshopper friend comes out from the kitchen area at one point and offers her support, which pumps us up a little. She won't sit down with us but she tells us she thinks what we're doing is cool.

When the bosses finally arrive they approach us with David sandwiched between the two district managers. We're all sitting with our backs to the windows so that they have to stand with their backs to the kitchen area where all the workers are pretending to work.

Brian launches into a tirade and it's clear this conversation will not go as well as our talk with David. I didn't fire you for calling in sick! I fired you because you haven't been committed to your job lately! We were going to make you a manager but then you started slacking off at work and complaining about your job. Rob and David add supporting arguments here and there. I'm trying to get a word in but failing.

Then something unexpected happens. Joe, who hasn't said a word to this point, pipes up out of nowhere and starts shouting. I've worked with Kate at Dinkytown and she works harder than anybody else there! She's been working 7 days a week for you guys and you won't even pay her a decent wage! She gets strep throat twice in one month and is trying to come into work anyway so that she can pay her bills and your response is to fire her!? You should be ashamed of yourselves! He goes on uninterrupted for about a minute and after that we control the conversation.

Brian and David go silent and for the rest of our talk it's the five of us versus Rob, who as the owner's son has the most authority of the three. He won't admit that they fired

Kate for calling in sick and he won't agree to rehire her. But he does cede to us that workers should receive warnings before they are fired, and nobody should get fired for calling in sick.

When we've made all our points and can't think of anything new to say, we share a look with each other. Time to go. We thank the bosses for meeting with us, then stand up and leave.

On the walk back to Kate's house we look towards the store and catch Rob outside lighting a cigarette. He doesn't smoke, so we must have rattled him pretty good.

Kate will soon decide that she doesn't want to fight for her reinstatement anymore. She had her chance to stick it to the bastards and that's enough for her.

The Riverside driver we gave the $80 tip had told me at the bar that if we carried out our plan we would all get fired. He witnessed the entire action, and I'm hoping that what we've done will make workers less fearful of confronting their managers.

As for me, I feel like a new person. I can now lump myself into that category of people who have risked losing their job to stand with their coworkers and confront the bosses. I guess I'm a union organizer now.

Chapter 6
Demeaning Work

June 23rd, 2007

Oh, Jamal also had me clean the display racks and wouldn't let Nick smoke. And he said "we gotta play by the rules now," as in they were going to start enforcing previously unenforced company policies, as a result of Monday's action.

When I first started working at Jimmy John's the two corporate policies that bugged me the most were uniforms and punch-lists.

For uniforms we wore black t-shirts with giant obnoxious slogans on the back. FREAKY FAST. MAYO MASTER.

23

VOTE JIMMY. Etcetera. We also wore JJ hats, blue jeans or khakis, black shoes, white socks, one optional ear piercing in each ear, and band-aids over our visible tattoos. Not exactly an outfit I'd wear out party-hopping.

The punch-lists were check-lists of daily cleaning and stocking tasks we had to sign off on after rush hours. I was raised to believe that when a trash can becomes full, you should empty it. Not so at Jimmy John's. There you emptied the trash after lunch, dinner, or bar rush, whether or not it was full. In the event that it was not yet time for cleanup but the trash filled up anyway, you let it overflow onto the floor. Drove me crazy.

But it's amazing what you can get used to, and after a few months working there I was tucking my shirt in and wiping down already-clean tables with the best of them.

A couple weeks after our action around Kate's firing, work got even more demeaning at the Dinkytown store. Our manager Jamal started making us "deck scrub[21]" every day. He wouldn't let inshoppers go out for cigarette breaks. He told us that "somebody must have pissed Rob off because Rob says I have to be an asshole to you now." I eventually got fed up and told him that the reason Rob was mad was because myself and several others were pissed at the Riverside manager and fucked up their store's business. I stopped short of threatening Jamal with direct action, but after I spoke up he backed off me anyway.

Really though Jamal was just trying to isolate myself and the others who had participated in the action. I remember my coworker Nick Consentino complaining loudly how "they gotta punish everybody for something just a few people did" and feeling a lot of hostility from him.

Turns out social ostracism at work can be scarier for an organizer than the threat of actually getting fired. Suddenly you're on your own hellish stressed-out island for your entire 10-hour shift. Your manager's pissed at you, and

---

[21] Pour some gnarly chemical shit on the tile floors and scrub

your coworkers are pissed at you because your manager's being a dick to them.

Ideally someone else on your shift has your back, in which case there's not much management can do. But in my case on Thursday nights I had no one to support me. So I just held my head high, picked my spots to confront them, and within a couple weeks it blew over and work went back to the level of demeaning to which we were all accustomed.

Chapter 7
Direct Action

June 14th, 2007

I'm aware that my role in the campaign has changed drastically. I think people are looking to me for direction now. I'm fine with taking on a leadership role, but I need to make sure to encourage other people to take their own initiative and lead their own actions.

I really want to finish Pudd'nhead #4, but I find myself growing obsessed with this campaign and have resigned myself to the fact that Jimmy John's may consume my summer.

Today I'm calling 1-on-1 Bikes, Kate, Jeff P., Wil, Jody, Joe, and everyone who works at Block E and Franklin and the few people I haven't talked to at Riverside. Talk about momentum!

My friend and fellow wob Nate once told me that direct action is the oxygen of an organizing campaign. If you don't organize actions the union gets stale and lifeless, but coming off an action everybody's fired up and excited to organize. Such was the case for us after the phone zap and march on the boss over Kate's firing.

While I was busy calling every JJ worker to warn them about possible tightening of rules, Jody spent the next week working on the first ever Jimmy John's bike race. We called it the "How Fast?" bike race and put fliers up in the back rooms of all 7 stores in the franchise. We set the race for the following Sunday and invited everybody whose phone number we had collected from the phone lists posted in the stores.

Only 7 people ran the race, but they represented all 7 stores in the franchise. Afterwards we had a party at the Belfry Center[22] with 15-20 JJ workers and various non-affiliated cool kids. My strongest memory of the party was Jody and I arguing with Jay Awesome in the parking lot at the end of the night, trying to convince him to come to meetings and help us organize a union.

A few weeks after the bike race we organized a scheduling action at the Dinkytown store. All the drivers came in to the shop and sat around a table in the dining area. We printed out an empty schedule and had a meeting in front of management to design our own schedule. Two drivers couldn't make it, but they called and told us what shifts they wanted.

We were overstaffed at the time and everybody wanted more hours, so the best we could do was share the pain in as fair a manner as possible. Seniority gave you priority for shifts and no one had more than 4 shifts a week or less than 2. We did actually add one shift to the schedule, which our manager never noticed.

Direct action is the foundation of the IWW's organizing model. It means organizing a group of people to directly confront an authority figure about a specific grievance. In union organizing you want to choose the lowest-level boss that can affect the changes you're seeking – in our case the store GM. The ultimate goal of any action is to empower workers by showing them that if we act together we can improve our working conditions and our lives.

After the meeting we submitted the schedule to our general manager. His response – "this is going to be the schedule from now on." Success!

I finally had a regular schedule. And I'd still be working those shifts long after everyone else who worked there – managers included – were gone.

---

[22] Collective anarchist art space at 38th and Bloomington

Chapter 8
The AFSCME Strike

December 30th, 2007

Max is going out of town in a day or two. I doubt he's appeared in this journal yet, but he once talked to me about getting a job at JJs. I remember I talked to somebody about him at the AFSCME picket (Max was at the 6am picket). I said he was interested in the IWW but he doesn't take anything seriously. I think I was wrong about that.

In the fall of 2007 three AFSCME locals representing workers at the University of Minnesota went on strike. Jimmy John's delivery drivers were biking past picket lines, and I was getting up at 5am to go walk a wobbly-organized picket and try to block delivery trucks.

AFSCME and the IWW were both legally considered unions, but organizationally they could not have been more different.

The leadership of AFSCME Local 3800 was dominated by members of a socialist group called Freedom Road[23]. Freedom Road's general strategy was to seek key positions in labor organizations or social movements and then lead the unknowing masses into revolutionary struggle. Thus AFSCME 3800 called two major strikes in a 4-year time-span, and they got their asses handed to them on both occasions.

The problem with AFSCME and other mainstream unions was that though they had thousands of members, being a member in AFSCME meant a hell of a lot less than being a member in the IWW. Typically it just meant you were covered by a collective bargaining agreement and you got union dues taken out of your paycheck.

I talked to a young woman at some party right before the strike. She told me she'd been getting emails from the

---

[23] I don't' mean to imply that leadership of most union locals belong to socialist political groups. I doubt that's the case, but it was with AFSCME 3800.

union and emails from the university and she didn't know who to trust. Though technically she was a member of the union, she'd never had any interaction with any of the union officials who were encouraging her to go on strike. It was clear to me that she viewed the union as a 3rd party and felt no affiliation to it. I call that paper membership. She was a member, but only on paper.

This lack of organization explains why after the AFSCME locals voted overwhelmingly to strike, only 30% of union members in those locals actually walked off the job. Most of them obviously had not participated in the voting.

My good friend and fellow wobbly Jeff P. was an AFSCME member at the U. He was critical of the AFSCME leadership's strike strategy. AFSCME wanted strikers picketing on visible street corners to garner public support. Then Democratic politicians would pressure the university to capitulate.

Jeff adhered to the IWW principles of direct action and worker control. He thought that to win the strike the workers would have to directly threaten the flow of goods to the university. To that end he enlisted his coworkers as well as local wobblies including yours truly to start our own picket line at the KYE docks on East River Road where trucks unloaded goods for the medical science buildings. This meant being down there between 5:30 and 8am when the trucks arrived.

Most of the time we lolled around smoking cigarettes and drinking coffee, chatting about the strike or Arrested Development or whatever. We had plenty of excitement though too.

After we turned a few trucks away[24], police and university lawyers descended on us like shitflies. Lawyers threatened us, cops argued with us, but ultimately we were within our rights and there wasn't a whole hell of a lot they could do.

_____

[24] Teamster drivers especially, who are not required to cross picket lines

The biggest excitement came when a truck tried to drive through our picket line and my friend Erik Davis refused to move. Instead he got a ride on the front bumper of this jackass's truck until my other friend Kieran caught up to the truck, opened the driver's side door, slammed on the brake with his hand, and pulled the driver out of his vehicle. Then came the shitflies.

Erik's unintended ride on the front of a truck notwithstanding, our tactics were so successful and popular with workers that at an assembly meeting AFSCME decided to endorse pickets of all the docks on the Minneapolis campus.

The pickets were nowhere near enough to win the strike, however, and after a couple missed paychecks the workers voted to accept the original university offer including wage and benefits cuts. As with most 21st century strikes in America, the union got pummeled.

I include this story to illustrate the difference between the IWW model of organizing and the entryist approach of various other radical left groups.

Freedom Road was a small socialist organization with far fewer members in the Twin Cities than the IWW. Yet by seeking key positions in a union bureaucracy they had been able to call thousands of workers out on strike. The vital step that this top-down approach to unionism missed was the actual organizing.

AFSCME was structured on the principle of paper membership. At some point in the distant past they had won exclusive collective bargaining rights for thousands of university workers, which meant those workers had to join the union and pay dues. But most AFSCME workers referred to the union as "them" and had never participated in the union on any level. On paper someone in that position is a union member. I would argue that practically speaking they are not.

It's hard to win a strike when your union members don't consider themselves union members. Impossible, really. It is my opinion that mainstream unionism's focus on collective bargaining rights and building paper membership at the expense of rank and file organization explains why unions in the United States have been losing strikes and declining in prominence for over half a century.

At Jimmy John's we were organizing with a bottom-up approach. We didn't want to win union recognition so that we could sign up a bunch of new members. We wanted to sign up a bunch of new members so that we could win union recognition. In the IWW we have a cliché for this approach: Organize the worker, not the workplace. Our focus was always on empowering ourselves and our coworkers. The goal was never to lead our coworkers into a strike. We wanted to organize our coworkers into a union so we could develop a collective action strategy together.

A month or two after the AFSCME workers went back to work, I attended a "Lessons of the Strike" panel discussion Freedom Road had organized. I sat incredulous and listened to Freedom Road members speak about this momentous moment for the labor movement, where thousands of enraged workers had taken to the streets and stood up for their rights. If I hadn't participated in strike actions and spoken with AFSCME members about their new contract, I would have thought the union had won.

You'll get no such rosy spin from me.

Chapter 9
The Calhoun Committee

September 16th, 2007

We drank beer the whole meeting (this at 5pm), Devo Eric, Grant, and Joe smoked spliffs. The substance use concerns me, but today it didn't seem like too much of a problem.

We talked about all our grievances for 45-60 minutes. Wages, hours, job security, dress code, same old shit.

We talked for ½ hour about how to organize. I felt like this could have gone better, but we hit the essentials. Direct action, basically. The Calhoun folks talked about organizing an action around reviews/raises. They were resistant to collective action tactics and wanted to confront their GM Krysta separately and individually. That annoyed me.

After Kate got fired we continued meeting at her house for a while, with meeting attendance between 3 and 5 people. But Kate was no longer at Jimmy John's and couldn't find a way to contribute to the union. She did make chili on behalf of the IWW for a cook-off, but the longer she was out of work the less interested she was in the campaign. Before long we stopped having regular meetings.

In September 2007, Wil finally had an organizing breakthrough at his store in Uptown. He had figured out how to do 1-on-1s and was getting all his coworkers excited about the union campaign. We started holding regular meetings again, this time at Wil's coworker Devo's house in Phillips.

Eric Corkoran was the most enthusiastic guy in that crew. He was a large chatty street punk[25] fellow with overactive eyes that always looked like they were about to leap out of his face. He joined the IWW immediately, attended an IWW organizer training, and shouted to anyone who would listen about the sad state of working conditions at Jimmy John's.

The Calhoun-centric committee meetings were fun but wildly unproductive. Lots of booze, weed, and rants. Very little in the way of concrete organizing tasks. We would talk casually about who we should approach next that might be down with the union, but few of us had any training setting up 1-on-1 meetings, so pretty much they never happened.

I think the reason we allowed alcohol and marijuana at our meetings was that we considered ourselves a different kind of union that didn't have to follow the rules like other unions. We were young minimum-wage workers obsessed with direct action and hostile to bureaucracy. We were mostly fuckups of one variety or another and we weren't embarrassed about it. So what if other unions had boring

---

[25] Punks with spikes who say "Oi" in 4/4 time and standard tuning.

meetings. Our meetings were going to feel like a party, and no one could tell us to operate any other way.

Of course, it's hard to conduct business at a party. That's a lesson we had to learn the hard way.

Nothing ever came out of our meetings and the workers at Uptown JJs never organized any actions. Nothing changed, and our meetings started to feel like just the same old drunken rants about low wages and disrespectful managers. By winter we had stopped meeting regularly again and most of the Calhoun workers had dismissed the idea of unionizing as an impossibility.

Chapter 10
Bicycle Delivery

December 30th, 2007

I was at a party at the Zombie House on 26th and Como like a month ago. I biked 5 miles there in the brutal cold (-10 F), made out with A-----, and talked organizing with Eric Corkoran, Jay, and this girl whose name I've forgotten but came to the Utah Phillips show and apparently talked to me about organizing like a year ago.

When I started working at Jimmy John's I didn't even own a bike. I'd been delivering pizzas for four years in a variety of mostly functional automobiles.

The problem with car delivery at JJs was that I wasn't making as much money in tips, because I was delivering $4 - $6 sandwiches instead of $15 - $20 pizzas. I couldn't afford maintenance on a full-time delivery vehicle, so with the help of Jody and the Grease Pit[26] I dove headfirst into the world of bicycle delivery.

My first road bike was a hefty blue Lotus. After an 8-hour shift delivering on that beast my ass felt like a burn victim and my legs were useless. For a while I considered it a

---

[26] Volunteer West Bank (at that time) bike repair collective

success just to make it through a night shift and still be able to pedal hard enough to make the wheels spin.

As fall turned to winter my ass adjusted to the bike seat and my thighs ballooned with muscle. I also became acquainted with hellish Minneapolis biking conditions. Freezing rain was the worst — in jeans it numbed my legs — but ice, subzero temperatures, and whiteout snow conditions were honorable mentions as well.

On the one hand I felt like I should be getting paid more than $6.75 an hour, given how much work I was doing and the danger inherit in dodging cars on a bicycle. But on the other hand I felt a sense of freedom and empowerment being able to bike anywhere and in any weather conditions.

My favorite challenge was speeding through the dense pedestrian traffic on campus during the school semester. It was like a real-life Pacman game where you had to focus on where each of the 30 or so pedestrians were headed and find where the gap would be by the time you reached them. Also you can take more chances dodging pedestrians than trucks because if you fuck up typically they don't kill you.

Another major benefit to becoming an avid biker was that it made it much easier for me to stop driving drunk, which I'd been prone to doing in years past. In those days I was going out every night — sometimes party-hopping between 3 or 4 parties in one night. Jimmy John's workers were all over the city and I wanted to talk to every one of them about my vision of America's first fast food workers union and how inspiring it would be to millions of underpaid food service workers.

I suppose I also wanted to get shitty drunk, act like a total jackass, and hook up with various ladies. I got better at that too.

Chapter 11
Turnover

August 26th, 2007

Uriah was fired/quit for some bullshit and Jamal gave his Monday and Tuesday nights to Courtney.

October 24th, 2007

Joe Blackseer got fired Wednesday for calling in sick. We had a meeting on Sunday at Jody's house to try to figure out how to get him his job back.

November 25th, 2007

Jody quit last night. I heard it from Tim. Jody did not talk to me or any other wobs or JJ folks about it. The son of a bitch has no phone, so I sent him a myspace message earlier today. Haven't heard back. So there goes my best friend at Dinkytown, and now Wil and I are the only survivors from the era of Kate's house meetings.

January 17th, 2008

JJ campaign seems dead currently. Fucking Eric Corkoran quit, without telling me. I'm going to beat the shit out of that motherfucker.[27]

Around the time of the Calhoun JJs influx to the committee, Joe Blackseer got fired for calling in sick.

Joe was a senior employee at the Dinkytown store. He was the guy who had spoken up during our confrontation with the district managers over Kate's firing. After that action it came out somehow that management had in their brilliance labeled Joe the masterminded of the whole action. So possibly they had been seeking an excuse to fire him for some time. And at Jimmy John's, contagious sickness was one of the top reasons to fire somebody.

We had a decently attended meeting about Joe's firing and ultimately set up a sit-down with DM Brian to protest the decision. By the time of the sit-down though, Joe had already found another job and didn't want to return. So instead of demanding his reinstatement we aired all our complaints about

---

[27] Eric outweighed me by several hundred pounds and I couldn't throw a punch to save my life. Thankfully drunken rants to your organizing journal aren't legally binding.

34

our GM Jamal, who was subsequently fired a couple months later for gross incompetence. Another result of that sit-down was that the three of us who participated – Jody, the new driver Courtney, and myself – all received the extra hours we wanted, and I started working two shifts a week at the Riverside JJs in addition to my Dinkytown shifts.

A month later Jody quit, and a month after that Eric Corkoran quit. With every committee member we lost, down sank the morale of our remaining committee members. By the end of 2007 the committee had shrunk back down to just myself and Wil, and we weren't meeting regularly[28].

The two most challenging aspects of trying to organize fast food are turnover and geography. Geography's a distant second.

A year into my employment every worker at the Dinkytown JJs who had been there when I was hired – including managers – had either quit or been fired. Everyone except for me.

The atrocious working conditions made it difficult to convince people to stay. Either they eventually got sick of cleaning cash registers and scrubbing toilets or they fell out of favor with some manager and got fired.

Unions are built on trust, and trust takes time to build. The hardest part of this campaign for me – harder than biking in freezing rain and getting mangled by students' cars – was watching friends leave the committee. As time went on I desensitized myself to losing friends, which was debatably more depressing than the rage and sorrow I experienced early in the campaign.

I saw a great contradiction of an industry screaming out for unionization – minimum wage, draconian scheduling, zero benefits, etc. – and yet impenetrable for unions due to massive turnover.

---

[28] Excepting that we lived at the same house and would share shitty beers and listen to punk rock records

35

At least that's the way I felt heading into 2008. The union drive that had once seemed destined for greatness was dead in the frozen water, and if we in all our cockiness couldn't pull it off, probably nobody could.

Still, I've never enjoyed losing, and I wasn't ready to call it quits just yet.

*

2008

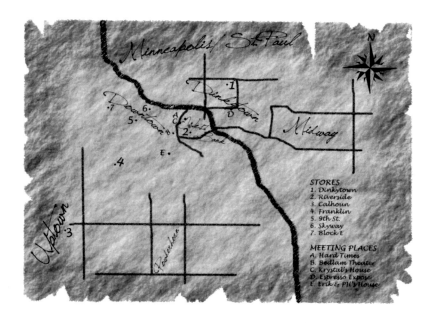

Minneapolis/St. Paul

N

Dinkytown

·1

Downtown

·7
6·
5·
A
C
8·
·2
West
Bank
D

Midway

E ·

·4

Uptown

Lyndale

Hennepin

·3

STORES
1. Dinkytown
2. Riverside
3. Calhoun
4. Franklin
5. 9th St.
6. Skyway
7. Block E

MEETING PLACES
A. Hard Times
B. Bedlam Theater
C. Krystal's House
D. Espresso Expose
E. Erik & PH's House

We just had a "meeting" at Krystal and Julia's. Basically we watched 4 episodes of "The Office." Wil showed up at about 9:30 after his Grease Pit meeting. He had forgotten about the meeting, which was disappointing.

Yesterday I trained in Pammy at Dinkytown. She's this U sophomore from Brainerd. She basically rode around in my car with me for 3 hours and it was awesome.

That night, even though I was dead tired/hungover, I went over to Pammy's friends' party. It was a goofy small college party. They had the Sci-Fi channel on and everybody was hanging out in this dinky living room. I talked to Pammy about organizing and she was way down. Said she'd come to the meeting today, but I couldn't get ahold of her.

I also went over to the Zombie House and picked up Wil and Jay Awesome, who I brought back to the college party. Talked a lot with Jay about organizing and various other topics. Jay hates Leo cause Leo's homophobic and calls Jay a fag.

Tuesday I went over to Jake from Skyway's apartment and drank vodka pineapple juices. Jake is trying to distance himself from the campaign. I talked with him quite a bit but was unable to sway him. We went to the CC Club and had a pretty awkward time where we didn't look each other in the eyes much. Then we went back to his apartment and I rambled about politics for a couple more hours.

Today showed up 2 hours late and drunk to this ExCo class on gentrification. Laila from Riverside and TJ from Dinkytown were both in attendance. I really wanted to talk about organizing but didn't on account of them both being there and being at different levels of in the know. I'm going to try to meet up with Laila this week.

Oh, I did call a St. Paul JJ tonight and get a confirmation that they start inshoppers at $7/hr.

Sara and Jody also said they'd come to the meeting today but didn't. Jody was sick. Leo was a maybe and Courtney said she was busy. Those were the calls I made.

According to Wil, sounds like we should be inviting Adam and Grant and maybe Abe to meetings. Chris D. got fired and Devo's in treatment for alcoholism. These are all Calhoun people.

I guess I have energy to do this again, but it's looking more impossible than ever. What else is new?

I'm not really sure what all this is going to take to get organized. But I'm hanging onto 6pm Sunday meetings from here on out. I don't even care. I'll go to Krystal's as long as she's PIC (which she is, at Riverside) and if she gets fired I'll go to somebody else's place.

Chapter 12
The Riverside Committee

Early in 2008 I started working more and more shifts at the Riverside JJs and eventually the only shift I had left at Dinkytown was my Saturday day shift I'd claimed in our scheduling action back in Summer 2007. This I did to combat the "Geography" problem I alluded to earlier.

By "Geography," I'm referring to how in 2008 our Jimmy John's franchise employed about 140 workers, but we were spread out in 7 different stores around Minneapolis. So even when we had an organizing breakthrough at say Dinkytown or Calhoun, the workers at the Riverside store weren't likely to even hear about it, let alone join us.

An inside organizing approach – where all the organizers work at the workplace in question[29] - leaves you two options to combat this geographic separation. Either you have organizers apply at the stores where you have no contacts, or if you're like me you pick up shifts at every store in the franchise and meet people that way.

When I started working at Riverside the union was completely off the radar for the 20-25 workers in that store.

---

[29] As opposed to an outside organizing approach, where union organizers do house visits with workers who are not their coworkers. Not evil, but different.

Within 3 months we were holding regularly scheduled meetings at my coworkers' apartment, and over 2008 the JJ organizing committee came to be dominated by Riverside workers. Krystal, Julia, Ashley, Pammy, Wes, Laila, Arnaldas, and myself. We also spoke with and swayed a majority of the other workers in the Riverside store to support the union.

Early in 2008 I was preaching small shop actions – specifically marches on the boss. We had some minor successes with these actions – the franchise bought us a bike trailer at Riverside and a couple managers started putting out tip jars – but we never had any significant victories and never organized any prose-worthy actions. Nevertheless, I had a blast working with those folks and felt much closer to them than I ever had with my coworkers at Dinkytown.

During that time I also became a regular at the Bedlam Theater[30] and Palmers bar on the West Bank. Krystal and I would bring sandwich platters to Palmers after we closed on Monday nights and trade them for free drinks[31]. There I had long passionate talks with all of my coworkers about work, women, the war, the world, you name it. Can't say I led any work stoppages or got anybody a raise though.

By Summer 2008 we began to lose momentum and people started moving away from the committee again. I decided that organizing around small shop-level issues was getting us nowhere fast, and it was time to move on to the franchise-wide issues and start circulating a petition for union recognition.

Chapter 13
A-E-I-O-U

May 23[d]*, 2008*

After the movie I went to Palmers and talked to Bobby a lot. He's staying with this girl who treats him like garbage (not saying he's any better – I have no idea), but he can't leave

---

[30] Specifically their happy hour bar

[31] Palmers is known for their stiff drinks, so I could get wasted just on a sandwich trade and save my money for the jukebox

her cause he'd be out on the street. He's a felon and can't get many jobs. His last job was through a temp agency, but then he got in a car accident. Now he has back problems and they won't take him back cause he's a workers comp liability. I think hanging out with us Wednesday was probably the highlight of his week. And even though he hits on girls nonstop, he's surprisingly kind to them in most situations.

I drove Bobby back to his house in Northside and drank a glass of water in his kitchen. There was a half-naked black boy sleeping on the couch in front of a turned-on TV. Bobby's girlfriend stayed in the bedroom and didn't meet me. Bobby says he's down for organizing and knows not to talk about it at work. Like everybody else, Bobby wants to leave town. And like some people, Bobby is suicidal.

The two barriers to workers coming together as a union are fear and futility. Either workers are afraid of the boss's response to the union or they're worried that the union will never come together and win better working conditions. All workers experience both fear and a sense of futility, to varying degrees, when they consider fighting back at work. The only way to break down those barriers is through collective action and intimate 1-on-1 conversations.

In the IWW and other grassroots organizations, we follow a loose model for how to carry out 1-on-1 conversations in which we try to up somebody's involvement in the organization. We call it A-E-I-O-U.

The first year of the JJ campaign I talked to maybe 50 of my coworkers about unionizing, but it wasn't until Spring of 2008 that I became confident in doing 1-on-1s with coworkers. I finally started setting up scheduled sober 1-on-1 meetings specifically to talk about work. Of course I also continued to talk shit at work, at bars, and at Monster Truck rallies. At this point I feel it's appropriate to introduce the A-E-I-O-U model, with organizing examples taken from my own experience.

A is for Agitate

I'm covering a shift at the Franklin store and it's pouring rain outside. The second driver arrives and he's soaking wet. He's a punk-looking dude with a leather jacket and a mohawk. The manager, who's a complete ass, sends him home to change his socks. They are white socks, the required color, but because they're so wet they look gray. I can't believe it. When he comes back half an hour later I introduce myself and start agitating him about this ridiculous sock issue. Did Mandel really send you home for having wet socks when you're doing bicycle delivery in the pouring rain? Does he always pull shit like that? How can you take that kind of abuse? His name is Stix and he's eager to tell me all about the insanity he has to deal with from management.

Like in the 12-step program of Alcoholics Anonymous, the first step to organizing is realizing that you have a problem. Agitating is not about you telling your coworkers what's wrong at work. It's about getting *them* to tell *you* what's wrong at work. And you can't stop there - you also have to ask *why* it's a problem, figure out the emotional element. So you don't get paid enough. Why do you care? What kind of monthly expenses are you struggling to pay? What happens if your check is short?

Agitation is the easiest step, especially at a shithole like Jimmy John's.

E is for Educate

I'm hanging out on the balcony at Krystal and Julia's apartment on Cedar and Riverside with a bunch of my coworkers from the Riverside store, drinking cheap beers and watching the snow melt. Bobby and Ashley are talking about how little they get paid. Bobby feels like shit about never having a dollar for the bus and always having to bum bus fare to get home from work. Well how do you think we could get raises for everyone? What if we staged a work stoppage in our store?

42

What if we did a work stoppage at all 7 stores? What if the entire city staged a work stoppage? Have you ever heard of the 1934 Teamsters Strike? It's been done before.

As in the 12-step program, the second step is admitting that some problems you are powerless to overcome by yourself. Educating is not about telling people what to do or how to do something, and it's not about teaching your coworkers the history of the labor movement. It's simply convincing people that collective action is the solution, and that as isolated workers we are powerless to solve any but the smallest of problems at work. You might be able to kiss enough ass to make 10% more than your coworker, but you can't make a fast food corporation offer a living wage.

I is for Inoculate

I'm sitting across a table from TJ at Hard Times, sipping my coffee in silence. TJ is such a unique character and 1-on-1s with him are unlike any others I've experienced. I've asked him if he thinks we'll get fired for organizing a union, and now I'm waiting for a response. TJ is a deep thinker and sometimes we'll sit for a whole minute without speaking before he offers his always-well-thought-out opinion. "I don't think they'll fire everybody, but I think once they catch wind of the union drive they'll try to fire anybody they see as a union leader." In contrast to TJ, I spit back the first thought that pops into my head. "I agree, but we still have some legal protection, and if we're organized well-enough before they fire us we can make it hell for them with direct actions that'll seriously fuck up their business if they decide to come after us, and also yada-yada-yada..."

Fear is the mind-killer and must be addressed. In union campaigns you specifically have to discuss retaliatory firings, which are a very real risk and in the back of everyone's mind. The more you understand and pre-plan responses to anti-union tactics, the less frightened everyone will be and the better you will be able to fight back. Besides firings, the other big issue I always liked to bring up was the company turning middle managers against the union and the nasty social divisions that could arise at work after the union went public.

O is for Organize

"Organize" in the A-E-I-O-U model specifically means delegating tasks, or getting someone to actively participate in the campaign. I still wasn't too good at this as of Spring 2008. More on that later.

U is for Union

The 'U' in A-E-I-O-U can really mean whatever you want it to, but for me it reminds me that Unions are all about building real connections with the people in your community. There's math and logic to organizing, no doubt, but ultimately it's the emotional bonds between us that make solidarity powerful. It's making their problems yours and your problems theirs[32].

I'm drinking 2-for-1s at the Dinkytowner with Leo. He's been working full-time at the Dinkytown store for about a year. He shows me his two week pay stub and it's $860 after taxes and child support. Leo's a small-time drug dealer who has been in and out of jail since he was a teenager. He has a daughter he loves and he's trying to go straight for her sake and get out of the drug trade, but he's not making enough money to support himself and he can't find any higher-paying work. He tells me that even if he could make 50 cents more an hour, maybe he could stop slinging Oxi. It breaks my goddamn heart.

---

[32] i.e. "An Injury To One Is An Injury To All"

44

Chapter 14
The Card Campaign

April 27th, 2008

Earlier today I was feeling awful, like the campaign was over. It's hard to keep seeing friends come and go. The old Dinkytown crew is all gone now. Jody, Leo, Joe, Marissa, Kate, Uriah, the Smiths – it's just me and Courtney and a bunch of fresh faces.

Sometimes when things are going good it's so close I can see it, I can almost touch it. I feel it happening and it's the best feeling in the world. But then somebody quits or loses the faith and it's just as impossible as it ever was.

But life goes on, and so does organizing. I don't think I'm ready to give up yet. So I don't think I will.

Every wobbly I had ever spoken with had warned me against NLRB[33] elections. The IWW organizer training put it something like this:

More than half of all recognition[34] campaigns never come to a vote. Either the union never gains enough support to petition for an election or they withdraw their petition before the election because of a brutal anti-union campaign.

Of those recognition campaigns where an election is actually held, 80% of the time the union loses the election.

Of those elections that the union wins, more than half of them never agree on a first contract[35] with the company. The only thing union recognition guarantees is that a union

---

[33] National Labor Relations Board – The government-appointed agency charged with administering the National Labor Relations Act. Union elections and unfair labor practices (ULP) disputes, basically.

[34] Union recognition is what the NLRB elections decide. You define a bargaining unit (x number of workers) and then they vote whether the union will be their collecting bargaining agent. As opposed to the status quo, where each individual worker negotiates the terms of their employment with their boss.

[35] Also known as a collective bargaining agreement, defines the terms of employment for all workers

45

can legally bargain with an employer on behalf of its members. It doesn't force the company to agree.

Taking a liberal estimate of a 3% success rate to the first contract, that contract still has a limited duration, after which you must negotiate a second contract. The company can also push a decertification petition, and at the end of the day it's a wonder collective bargaining agreements exist at all.

I'd also read a pamphlet by the Portland wobblies called "Learning From Our Mistakes" that had been influential within the IWW. It analyzed several of the Portland branch's campaigns in the years immediately before I'd joined the IWW. They had been the largest, youngest, and most inspiring branch in the union. Then a bunch of their campaigns collapsed and their membership shrank. Their conclusion: we should not have participated in the NLRB recognition process.

With that introduction, here's how I decided that the Jimmy John's campaign in Minneapolis should file for an NLRB election:

I was cocky

So everybody loses union elections. Whatever. We won't.

Our current campaign was failing

Our strategy of pushing single shop direct actions didn't seem to be working. By Summer 2008 we were going on our 3rd iteration of our organizing committee. In each iteration it had been dominated by workers in one store and eventually shrunk down to a few solid organizers when everyone else failed to see a way for JJ's to be a union job. First it was Dinkytown, then Calhoun, and now the Riverside committee was falling apart too.

We Needed Legitimacy

It's hard to believe in something that's never been done before, like say a union at a fast food franchise in the

United States. Nobody knew or had ever heard of or could even Google what it would look like, because it didn't exist yet.

Add to that we were young sex-crazed alcoholic potheads[36] with a lot of smarts but very little experience. Plus our union the IWW was small and radical and for the most part suit-less[37]. We needed some external legitimizing force to make our dreams become real possibilities to our coworkers.

We Needed a Decisive Victory

At the risk of exposing my inner math nerd, I'll say that revolution is not a goal, it's a process. There is no perfect society, there's only change. Society can become infinitely more ideal, or it can become infinitely more repressive. There is no end of the line.[38]

Likewise, a union can never win, we can only fight. I guess if you take over a company (or city, state, world, etc) you might not have the old bosses to fight anymore, but it'll never be perfect and revolutionary struggle will always exist[39].

Still I felt we needed to create that illusion of "victory." We needed a decisive symbolic victory that would inspire workers to fight back and more importantly would convince a shitload of people that the crazy idea we were pushing wasn't actually crazy – it was possible.

If we won a union election, workers in restaurants all over the country and probably the world would be contacting us trying to figure out how we did it and how they could organize their own workplaces. That was my belief.

---

[36] Some combination of the three, usually.

[37] My terse 40,000 foot view history of the wobblies: Big deal in the first ½ of the 20th century, notable members all imprisoned/killed, declined into obsolescence 50s-80s, in the late 90s applied solidarity unionism to retail and service industry campaigns and became relevant again. Still very small, still no expensive-suit-wearing high-powered labor lawyers or union bureaucrats.

[38] I swear that's based on calculus.

[39] See every major revolution in the history of humanity for examples

I also believed it would give incredible momentum to the 150 workers in our own franchise, so that we could finally pull off a franchise-wide action, like a work stoppage. Which would in turn win us the concrete gains in working conditions that the NLRB could of course never give us, like raises and health care.

I started pushing the idea of a recognition campaign in Spring 2008 and by Summer what was left of our committee had agreed. We designed and printed our own authorization cards, which we would present to our coworkers to sign. When a large enough majority of coworkers had signed authorization cards, we would file for a union election.

UNION YES!

I, _____, an employee of Miklin Enterprises/Jimmy John's, at the _____ location, am signing this card to authorize the Industrial Workers of the World to represent me and negotiate for better wages, hours and working conditions.

_____   _____
signature   date

_____
address

_____   _____
phone   e-mail

Our right to organize is protected by federal law. Any retaliation from the company is illegal.

Chapter 15
The RNC

August 28th, 2008
The RNC is in a couple days and I think I'm freaking out about it. These could be the largest political

demonstrations in the Twin Cities in my lifetime, and I've been on the sideline for the past year because I wanted to focus on this Jimmy John's campaign.

But the fact of the matter is I'm not doing shit right now. I haven't written a guitar riff in months, I haven't written for SSAAC[40] in months, I've written one song over the past 3 months, and my union activity has dropped to its lowest level since I wrote Pudd'nhead #4 two summers ago.

What else? I've been drinking like a fish. The only time I slow down is when I'm gambling. I was considering sobriety tonight, but I doubt that'll happen.

I think I might stare off into space the rest of the day and work on lyrics.

In 2008 the Bush/Cheny era was finally coming to a close, and the Republican party had chosen St. Paul as the site for their National Convention where they would nominate John McCain and Sarah Palin as the Bush/Cheny successors.

Long before the convention, an anarchist collective called the Welcoming Committee had formed in order to coordinate protests at the convention. I had joined the Welcoming Committee in Spring 2007 but dropped out in Fall of that year, a full year before the convention.

As a teenager I listened to punk rock and read such anti-capitalist staples as The Pearl by John Steinbeck and Scam by Iggy Scam. I was so dissatisfied with the state of the world that I started a punk band and played shows in various living rooms and garages around my hometown.

After high school I went off to college and took a bunch of history and political science classes. I read the Price of Glory by Alistair Horne and Coming of Age In Mississippi by Anne Moody. I was so outraged by war and oppression that I wrote several papers about it, for which I received excellent grades.

---

[40] Secret Society of Ape and Coffee. Writing group I belonged to 2007-2008. It was not so secret.

All by way of saying I didn't really get into the world of activism until I joined the IWW after college. And for a couple years I was pretty excited about it. I volunteered at two anarchist spaces, I went to classes organized by the Experimental College, I ate shitty Food Not Bombs dinners, and I even hopped a train[41].

When the Welcoming Committee formed, I was hesitant to join because I didn't see the practical purpose of protesting the convention. But I was easily convinced by my friend Erik Davis that we shouldn't allow the Republicans to take over the Twin Cities for the purpose of promoting their elitist agenda. Or at least we should make some sort of effort to disrupt it.

Early on in my Welcoming Committee career I remember writing an e-mail in which I suggested that "Shutting Down the Convention" should not be a goal of the Welcoming Committee. My two reasons:
1. It was unrealistic. We didn't have the capacity and people would only get disheartened.
2. Why bother? They'd just hold it somewhere else.

I must have had some alternate goals in mind when I wrote that, but they're not coming to mind right now. It probably should have been obvious to me that I had no business organizing protests that I felt had no practical objective. So there's that.

But also through my experiences in the Welcoming Committee and other anarchist collectives I came away with two major critiques.

First was the disconnect between the egalitarian rhetoric and the actual power structures within anarchist organizations.

The Welcoming Committee had large meetings, often of 30 or more people. The meetings had a rotating facilitator and used a consensus decision-making process. The Welcoming Committee had no officers or official leaders, so supposedly

---

[41] It was the wrong train. But I had a blast hitch-hiking from Iowa to Madison, the other train's destination.

everyone had an equal say in the decision-making. In actuality, those were the least democratic meetings I've ever attended.

The majority of the people at the meetings never said anything, except maybe during introductions when they divulged their opinions on vegetables[42]. All strategic decisions were made by 3 or 4 of the loudest and most opinionated participants. Even unpopular ideas were accepted, because we never voted on anything. The question wasn't, is this what you want? Instead it was, how much don't you want this? Enough to block it? If not, then let's do it.

In my opinion, any social structure of more than 10 or so people will develop power dynamics. You can recognize these dynamics and try to institute democratic safeguards. Or you can pretend they don't exist, in which case the most ambitious minority will come to dominate your organization[43].

Second was the trend in anarchist circles to glorify small affinity-group structures over mass organizations and mass movements.

Intuitively for me, all the major gains the 99% have won in human history were a result of mass struggle. In recent American history we have desegregation, the weekend, women's suffrage, minimum wage, and countless other victories of the labor movement in the 1890s and 1930s and the Civil Rights Movement of the 1960s.

But even in my own experience, I'll take 100 well-organized wobblies over 1000 unorganized sympathizers any day.

I remember going to the State Capitol in 2006 to protest the traveling anti-immigrant Minutemen. I was standing on the capitol steps with a few wobbly friends and a couple hundred total strangers. Down on the street in front of the capitol, six or seven Minutemen sat astride their sleek

---

[42] i.e. "Say your name and your favorite vegetable"

[43] I'm by no means the first person to reach this conclusion. Try *The Tyranny of Structurelessness* by American feminist Jo Freeman for a deeper exploration.

motorcycles with their hot girlfriends. They shook their booties at us and gave interviews to reporters, then left without incident.

I felt like the 250 of us had just been shown up by a handful of famous racists. If we were organized enough to even just surround them instead of all standing on one side of them, it would have felt more powerful. Alas, all we did was chant along to whatever the folks with megaphones chanted.

The contemporary theory behind large protests is more-or-less the same. Let's get as many people together as possible and have them do whatever the hell they want.

On the dawn of the Iraq War, for instance, we saw the largest protests in the history of humanity. Of course the war still happened, and the protests accomplished nothing.

In any event, I skipped the RNC except for the Rage Against the Machine march, and I felt fairly guilty about it. It was a way sexier brand of activism than organizing a fast food union. Hot young activists from all over the world were swarming south Minneapolis, and I didn't have a whole lot to say to them.

We also had about 20,000 cops in town, which sucked. Six squad cars broke up a basement punk show. Cops smashed down doors and woke my friends up by sticking automatic rifles in their faces. Eight members of the Welcoming Committee got charged with terrorist conspiracy and were facing up to 20 years in jail. And, of course, the convention went off without a hitch.

I started getting pretty disillusioned with anarchist activism.

Chapter 16
0 = Organize

July 8th, 2008

I ended up making the JJ authorization cards by myself.

52

July 20th, 2008

Left early for Dinkytown JJ parties. First at Angela from Franklin's house. Derbied bikes in the living room, talked work to Marrisa and rode the streets of Dinkytown with her sidesaddle and screaming on my bike.

Then to Emily from Riverside's friend's party. Soldiers, "rich bitches," a kiddy pool filled with chocolate and whipped cream. Made some friends, kicked the pool at some fool and got him all sticky.

July 24th, 2008

I biked around Minneapolis with Stix flyering Starbucks's. Pretty fun, but exhausting. Stix did well – he's a natural agitator.

Monday night at work was a nightmare – 2 deliveries in 8 hours and we ran out of lettuce, tomatoes, onions, roast beef, vito meat, and bread (3 times!). But I did set up meetings with Courtney and Krystal. Sadly Krystal is flaking out as I write this – we were supposed to meet up now.

August 17th, 2008

Organizing is all but dead again, just as I feared. Doesn't seem anybody did anything at JJ while Terracide was on tour. So we have a meeting today and need to get things rolling again. I expect it'll be me, Wil, Arnaldas, and Stix, which is basically our committee now. I think I'll talk about the 'O' in A-E-I-O-U.

September 28th, 2008

I've had a sense that the campaign is over, and it's killing me. If nothing else, I want to go out with a bang. I don't want to quit like this. Not after all I've put into this campaign.

I spent all summer meeting up with JJ workers and getting them to sign authorization cards. I agitated, I educated, and I inoculated. I went to a hundred different parties and got bug-eyed drunk hollering about wage slavery and radical unionism. I did loads of formal 1-on-1s at coffee shops, sometimes 2 or 3 in a day, where I talked to my coworkers about my vision for a union at Jimmy John's.

In retrospect, all that misguided energy damn near killed the campaign.

The 'O' in A-E-I-O-U — Organize - means delegating tasks. Once you are agitated and come around to the idea of collective action as a solution, you need to take on some task for the campaign. Until you take this step you remain a passive supporter, which doesn't count for much.

Early in the JJ campaign I was easily the most active committee member, but I was never the only one carrying out the work of the committee.

But as time went on and especially when the primary task of our committee in my mind became meeting with our coworkers and asking them to sign authorization cards (a passive act), I began to shoulder more and more of the responsibility for the campaign.

I was the only member of our committee who felt comfortable in a 1-on-1 talking about the union. I tried doing 2-on-1's with other committee members to make them more comfortable but it was still me driving the conversation and nobody else ever started setting up formal 1-on-1's of their own initiative. Of the 40 or so cards people signed in that initial push, I was present for about 30 of them.

The hardest organizing lesson for me to learn was that you cannot organize a union by yourself. You can be the most passionate righteous charismatic individual in the world or a selfish beer-bellied bully and it really doesn't matter — individuals are powerless to organize unions.

I was meeting with every coworker I could reach to try to convince them to passively support our union, and I had great success. But every month our committee got smaller and less motivated. I remember one day in October when Arnaldas — a smooth-talking and disciplined Lithuanian delivery driver at Riverside who had become a solid excited committee member — asked me: "Is it even worth it?"

Wil wanted to quit. Laila — the thrifty over-educated survivalist / Riverside delivery driver who had won us the bike

54

trailer at Riverside – did quit. Arnaldas was still down but doubting. And I felt like the more I tried the worse off we were.

The one exception to this trend was Stix – that mohawked thrill-seeker I had worked with at Franklin whom Mandel had sent home for having wet socks. Stix and I flyered and talked union (an active act) at a bunch of Starbucks's in July when the Starbucks Workers Union[44] went public in the Twin Cities. I gave Stix a stack of authorization cards and he quickly got all the delivery drivers at his store to sign them.

Stix was our most jazzed up committee member, but he had severe drug, alcohol, and overworking habits that made him unreliable about attending meetings. Still, when I finally gave the campaign up for dead and quit Jimmy John's, it would be Stix who brought me back.

Chapter 17
Obama

November 6th, 2008
Obama's our president elect as of Tuesday night, and turns out I'm depressed by it. Tuesday I went barhopping with Savannah and Wil. Everyone was going nuts on the West Bank. I felt so alienated.

As both a radically-minded critical thinker and an argumentative belligerent drunk, I've long considered myself a high risk for becoming a wingnut. To me the difference between a wingnut and a radical is that a wingnut cannot root their arguments in practical experience.

Say you have a hypothesis that cell phones cause cancer. A wingnut will hear all the arguments in favor of the hypothesis, decide that they make good logical sense, then go around preaching that radio waves from smart phones are the harbingers of the apocalypse. A radical would reserve judgment until somebody actually got cancer from a cell phone.

---

[44] An IWW production

55

Around the time of the RNC, just as the underground Minneapolis scene was getting fired up about anarchists and cops, an alternate trend was emerging as well – everyone in my life fell in love with Barack Obama.

Barack Obama was attractive, well-spoken, not George W. Bush, and more importantly – he was black.

The one-word motto of the Obama campaign was "HOPE," and almost everyone I knew bought into it. Even many of the anarchists marching in the Red and Black Bloc at the RNC protests were excited to have Obama as a president. A popular funny chant at the time: "Abolish! The State! Obama in '08!"

I was conflicted. On the one hand I too felt it was a great step forward. It felt like progress for the American people – a sign that for a majority of people skin color no longer mattered like it once had.

But the man himself I did not trust. For every presidential election since I could vote I'd been saying the same things. These candidates are both members of the ruling class elite, and they both represent the interests of ruling class motherfuckers who have nothing in common with me. They're 2 of 100 U.S. Senators in the world, or they're 2 of 50 U.S. Governors. Neither of them are anti-war. They're just arguing about who's going to send *more* troops into combat. This was true in 2004 (pro-war former Governor versus pro-war U.S. Senator) and it was still true in 2008 (pro-war U.S. Senator vs. pro-war U.S. Senator).

It's not that I thought Obama was an evil person. Hell, I didn't even think Bush was evil, and for that matter I never thought that the owners of my Jimmy John's franchise were evil either[45]. In their minds they were probably doing the right thing most of the time, it's just that the right thing for them was almost never the right thing for me.

---

[45] Jimmy John himself I do consider evil. He hunts endangered species. I can't get down with that.

The first line of the IWW Constitution's Preamble is "The working class and the employing class have nothing in common." Whenever I signed somebody up to the union I always went over that sentence and stressed the part about *class*. It's not that we as individuals have nothing in common. It's that classes have inherently different interests. At work – you have an incentive to make as much money and do as little work as possible, whereas the owner has incentive to pay you as little money for as much work as possible.

The same goes for the United States government. It's not that the individuals are evil, it's that the structures are undemocratic. There are no cooks in Congress, and there are no nurses on the Supreme Court. It wouldn't seem to me that millionaires and billionaires are more qualified to decide issues like going to war than you or I, but that's the America in which we live.

That's how I felt, but I couldn't find a way to express myself in terms of practical experience that made any sense. And in the meantime all my friends were drunk on Obama, seeing visions of world peace and equality. On election day I got a text from my friend and former coworker Leo, whom I'd always considered apolitical. He implored me to vote for Obama and "Change The World!"

Honestly I hadn't decided even as I walked to my polling place. I wanted to be a part of the excitement, and I did feel optimistic about electing our first President of color.

But when I got in the booth I couldn't do it. Fuck that. I voted on the local offices and referendums and wrote in my roommate for President. I can't vote for some millionaire U.S. Senator to make decisions on my behalf.

That night I went barhopping on the West Bank with my good friends Savannah and Wil. We watched the election results and drank the free beers to which our "I Voted" stickers entitled us.

At the end of the night I was sitting outside in the Palmers patio, shitty drunk, watching the party. The entire West Bank community was dancing in the middle of Cedar

57

Avenue. The punks from Medusa, the Somalis from the high rises, hippies from Riverside Park, the bike club, bartenders, drunks, convicts, cabbies, kids — pick your social group — they were there. Everyone singing, slapping hands, screaming "We did it!" and "Here's to hope!"

I stayed inside the fenced-in back patio at Palmers, sipping my whiskey, thinking maybe I was the crazy one.

Chapter 18
Quitting

November 6th, 2008

Today was supposed to be my last day at JJ, but I got Courtney to cover my shift. I'm sick. Probably because I've been drinking heavily and not eating.

Tuesday was really stressful at work. Arthur cried. Griffin and Ryan argued about everything. We were super-busy. I was deathly hungover. I wanted to quit so bad. I ended up telling Ryan I "needed some time off." So now I'm on indefinite hiatus.

Really this is the lowest I've felt in a long time. I have no plans, no prospects, no love. No clue what to do with myself.

So I guess this is my last JJ journal entry. I'm quitting the campaign and I feel like absolute garbage about it. It's like breaking up with someone you love. I've breathed JJ for the past year and a half. I don't know what to do now. Maybe I'll go vegan.

In September 2008 Wil finally gave up and quit Jimmy John's to go travel around the country. That left our committee as myself, Arnaldas, and our coworker Ashley, who had attended meetings but had never taken an active role in the campaign. Within a month I had lost all hope of unionizing our franchise and resolved to quit before the end of winter. Then one hellish understaffed rainy shift in November I snapped and put in my one-week notice.

I never had any plans for life after Jimmy John's, so I just did what came naturally: I gambled and drank and had lots of sex with a girl who was dating somebody else[46].

If I wasn't at the casino playing poker I was biking around on icy streets with 15 beers in my bag, looking for a place to get obliterated. Minneapolis has a lively underground beer and cocaine scene[47], so finding parties never presented much of a challenge.

Ever since I was 18 I've had a problem with gambling – poker specifically, but I'll place a bet on just about anything. And I've gone on some pretty good runs.

Once I won at least $200 on 10 consecutive trips to the casino. A couple new poker concepts had finally clicked for me, and I thought I'd figured it out and would never have to work again. It was like a weight had lifted off my shoulders that I'd never even known was there. I was free! No more prepping mayonnaise, no more mandatory meetings about tucking in my shirt, no more pretending to be busy when the owner was around. I didn't even need an alarm clock! Until I started losing...

We all are going to have to work for most of our lives – say 50, 60 years. At least everybody I know will. In most cases we'll be making somebody else rich and struggling to pay our own bills. It's this bummer we call capitalism.

You can accept this, keep your head down, put in your 100,000 hours at work, and try not to get too worked up about it.

Or you can fight against it, organize unions and other communities to try to change the way the world operates.

Or finally you can try to escape it, by say buying Powerball tickets or studying poker.

---

[46] It was an "open" relationship. As in weird and unfulfilling but with great sex.

[47] a.k.a. "the music scene"

Of the three options, organizing against capitalism to me seems the most fulfilling way to make it in this world, but trying to escape it via Texas Hold 'Em is awfully tempting.

Turned out that in November 2008 I was not yet a master poker player, and within two weeks I had blown the $1200 in my bank account and was flat broke. So I got a job shoveling snow at a couple corporate buildings in St. Louis Park. I was on call working overnights and I hated it.

My involvement in the Jimmy John's campaign had been the most fulfilling part of my life for almost 2 years, and I'd had such elaborate dreams of what we could accomplish. I thought we'd win union recognition, completely change the working conditions in our stores, spur organizing at other restaurants around Minneapolis, and spread our campaign to other JJs around the country. Letting go of that dream crushed me.

But I didn't have any other great ideas for what to do with my life, and I wasn't getting enough hours at my snow-shoveling gig, so without much fanfare I returned to work at Jimmy John's after just 3 weeks away. I was only working one 4-hour shift a week, and I had no intention of organizing. But I was back.

Chapter 19
Uninspiring Committee

November 25th, 2008

I'm back at Dinkytown JJ, if only barely. I'm working Saturdays again, and I covered a 4-hour shift today. I think I've gained a little weight since I quit, so if nothing else, this should help my figure.

PH from Block E is living with Erik Forman now and has joined the IWW. The two of them set up a JJ meeting last night at their house. It was the three of us plus Stix and Arnaldas. We accomplished very little, in my estimation. Two important things to come up were:

1. New store open in St. Louis Park. I'm supposed to check it out.

2. Erik's unsurprisingly pushing for us to go public with a minority union. I didn't speak against it, but I have very little interest in it.

This is definitely the ugliest committee we've had yet. Four nerdy delivery dudes, plus a couple scrawny white wobblies. Suffice it to say I'm not convinced this is heading in a positive direction.

Still, people are trying, and as long as the campaign has life, I guess this is what I ought to be doing. To be honest I had a couple really wretched weeks after I quit, and I didn't feel better until I went back to work.

After I returned to work at JJs I received several phone calls from my friend the industrious Starbucks Union organizer, Erik Forman. He wanted to put together a union meeting for Jimmy John's workers. He felt that wobblies had put too much time and soul into the campaign to let it fizzle out and die. I in contrast felt that it already had fizzled out and died.

Erik and I had started our organizing careers at about the same time – him at Starbucks and me at Jimmy John's. We'd both seen our organizing committees come together again and again only to dissolve as committee members burnt out or got fired. We'd both learned how to do solid 1-on-1's, and we'd both participated in successful job actions.

We used to joke about making a Union Organizing role-playing game where you did such glamorous work as making phone calls and sitting around at coffee shops. You'd roll dice to see if people answered your calls, stood you up for 1-on-1's, said they'd come to a meeting but flaked out at the last second, and so on.

Erik and I also started our respective campaigns with our respective best friends. And we both watched our best friends burn out and quit. Erik somehow made it through that and continued advocating for the union at Starbucks. For me it had been too much. The campaign was dead, I had no energy left for organizing, and I did not want to attend any union meeting.

But then my friend Stix called me and talked me into it. He was still excited about the Jimmy John's union, even if nobody else was. He told me I didn't have to commit to doing anything, but I should just come to the meeting and participate. So I did.

The first meeting we had that winter was 4 JJ workers – Stix, Arnaldas, PH, and myself – plus Erik Forman. After that, attendance declined. We met throughout November and December. I remember one particularly agonizing meeting that was just Erik, PH, and me. PH was a wealthy suburban implant to the city whose co-workers at the Block E store considered a wealthy suburban implant to the city. We sat around a card table in Erik's apartment at 15th and Franklin and probably discussed something but I wasn't that engaged. By January we had quit meeting again.

As 2008 ground to a close, I was back slapping mayo on French bread 16 hours a week but still working the occasional overnight snow-shoveling shift. Our committee had ceased functioning, and I began to wonder if it was impossible to organize during a Minneapolis winter. Two years in a row winter had killed our campaign, it seemed.

I still wanted a union election though, and I began talking to my coworkers about it again. I decided that I would dedicate whatever meager organizing efforts I had left in me towards the goal of holding a union election at Jimmy John's. Win or lose, nothing could be as bad as quitting and wandering around in a fog of futility.

*

2009

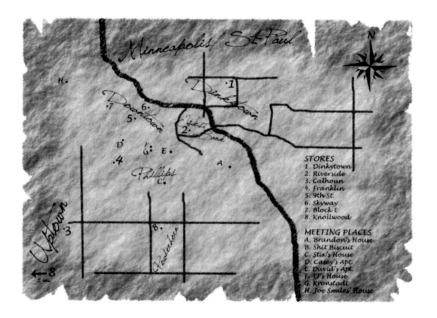

Minneapolis / St. Paul

N

1 Dinkytown

H.

Downtown

7. 6.
5.

2. West Bank

D. F.
G. E.
.4

Phillips
C.

A.

STORES
1. Dinkytown
2. Riverside
3. Calhoun
4. Franklin
5. 9th St.
6. Skyway
7. Block E
8. Knollwood

Watown

.3

8.

Radisson

MEETING PLACES
A. Brandon's House
B. Shit Biscuit
C. Stix's House
D. Casey's Apt.
E. David's Apt.
F. TJ's House
G. Kronstadt
H. Joe Smiles' House

← 8
2 mi.

February 16th, 2009

After the meeting we went to Tracy's for ½ price burgers. I drank 2 pints, which had absolutely no effect on me. I think that's a sign that I've been drinking way too much.

Yesterday for instance I drank from 2pm to bar close. Started out at the Bedlam during this playwriting workshop that Savannah tricked me into attending, then Kait, Wil, and I went to the Holiday Inn and drank there for four hours, then Savannah showed up. We finished the night at Palmers. I spent $50 on drinks and food yesterday. But I had good company.

I've been agitating at work a lot lately. I was even trying to agitate Wil last night. My plan for the next week is to just agitate as much as I can.

Chapter 20
Crazies

Back in Fall 2008 during one of his 11-hour late night delivery shifts, Arnaldas was smoking a cigarette behind the Riverside JJs when he struck up a conversation with one of the new guys. Arnaldas asked, what do you do? I like to play punk rock, and I hop trains, and I organize unions. Oh yeah? What union are you in? The IWW. Uh, what!?

The worker who casually claimed to be an IWW organizer was Brandon, and at the time our committee found this very alarming. Mostly because we were trying to keep our union organizing activities secret around the shop. We didn't want random weirdos casually discussing it with whomever.

But also I was very active in the Twin Cities IWW and had never met this guy. If he actually was a wobbly he hadn't been around long. Otherwise he was either lying or crazy. Our coworkers generally considered him crazy, and he got fired after only a couple months on the job. Our committee did nothing in his defense.

Brandon was not the first coworker of mine to casually mention the IWW at work. Back in late 2007 to Spring 2008 I had worked with this supposed anarchist "Star" whose W-2 name was Mica.

My first day working with Mica we tag-teamed a several-platter order to 7 Corners[48]. During that bike ride he told me that he knew all about the IWW organizing campaign at Jimmy John's, but that it wasn't going to work and really we needed to contact a different union. What a horse's ass. I yelled at him right then and got him to back off, but afterwards I always dreaded working with him.

Everybody at work thought Mica was an arrogant jerk. But he knew about the campaign, so I felt like I couldn't completely ostracize him lest he turn rat and run to management. I danced that line for several months. Mica came to one meeting but was never the face of the union. Eventually he quit, and I celebrated.

An even crazier primitivist-anarchist type who worked at the Riverside store was TS. A majority of our organizing committee knew him from either the punk or activist scene. He had made news at the RNC for getting the shit kicked out of him by cops. I knew him as an attention-freak who really wanted to be a druid and teach me about chi.

At Riverside all our coworkers immediately decided TS was crazy when he threw a fit about having to wear socks at work. TS expressed interest in helping with the organizing campaign, but we were terrified of having him associated with the union. We kept him at arm's length and in short order he was fired.

During all this time, I myself was battling heavy depression with whiskey and beer. I would occasionally gamble myself into debts I couldn't pay back. And the rest of my waking hours I spent either working at Jimmy John's or talking to Jimmy John's workers about working at Jimmy John's. All by way of saying that I don't necessarily exclude myself from this category of "crazies," and I'm not entirely proud of having pushed away well-meaning workers.

---

[48] Neighborhood of the West Bank up around Cedar-Washington. A bunch of bars, but just a shadow of the destitution and debauchery that used to be Minneapolis's skid row.

Union organizing is half mutiny and half high school popularity contest. When approaching workers, you're looking for the popular kids who hate their boss. Problem is, workplace leaders often get preferential treatment from management, and it's the nerds and misfits who usually have the most complaints.

There's no way around it though – you have to get the leaders on your side. A leader is somebody who has followers. If you ignore leaders and organize with crazies, then when the mutiny occurs, those leaders will come out as anti-union and turn all their followers against the union too. Thus union organizers tend to focus on long-tenured workers with the cushier jobs and ignore newer "crazier" workers. In other words, we often have to decide between compromising our ideals and doing what intuitively seems best for the campaign.

In early 2009, Brandon – who kicked off this chapter on crazies during a cigarette break with Arnaldas – was rehired and started working at the Calhoun store in Uptown. He was eager to jump right into the campaign and try his hand at union organizing. I had my concerns, but...

The campaign had felt dead to me for quite some time. I'd already quit, and I was no longer that concerned about management discovering my union sympathies and firing me. Most of my managers already knew I was trying to organize a union anyway[49]. At least if I got fired I wouldn't feel guilty about quitting. What I feared most was the campaign fizzling out and dying a dull death. I wrote in my journal at the time that maybe what we needed was some crazy.

Brandon immediately became active in our organizing committee and we started having regular meetings again. He was a controversial figure at his store but made several friends there too, including Andy Culling. Andy also started attending meetings and became active in the committee.

Brandon wanted to organize a job action. He had been agitating around this asshole manager Josh. Josh was your

_____

[49] Either I'd told them before they got promoted or somebody else had.

typical disrespectful manager - gave orders instead of asking nicely, took pride in making workers get down on their knees and scrub, etc. Brandon and Josh hated each other. It wasn't long before the situation came to a head.

Chapter 21
The Uptown Work Stoppage

March 23rd, 2009
I find myself smiling less and less, especially during union meetings. Just now Iain was at Hard Times and I laughed at some joke of his, thinking I was being sincere. Then I think we both realized I wasn't. I was just being nice. Suffice it to say, I'm in a bad mood.

Lots of shit's happening at JJ though. Yesterday I was working at Dinkytown and I got a call from Brandon. "Guess what just happened to me?" he said. "You got fired," I said. "My manager just hit me." Apparently it was over him and Jay (who I don't know) cutting the sandwiches diagonally.

He asked me what he should do, and I asked who he was working with. He said Andy and this guy Jay. I said well if you can get everyone to stop working, then do it and call up Rob. He said, "We're not working until Joshua (PIC) gets fired." Thus started the Uptown JJ work stoppage.

After Brandon told me he was calling a work stoppage in Uptown, I spent the rest of my shift frantically calling and texting union members and friends and encouraging them to head to the Uptown store and support the work stoppage. Saturdays were my busiest shift at work[50], so luckily I was out of the store distributing sandwiches and had the freedom to talk on the phone. I occasionally paused to do my job.

When I arrived in Uptown after finishing my shift, I found 25 or so people crowded in front of the store. Brandon was talking to the cops, and Andy was standing in his apron

---

[50] Which actually had nothing to with business and everything to do with staffing – I was the only driver.

with his arms crossed, next to the front door. Grant and Rory, two workers who had arrived to work the night shift, were hanging out in front smoking cigarettes, waiting for the work stoppage to end. The manager was inside working feverishly and avoiding eye contact.

From what I heard, the action went something like this:

- Brandon calls Rob Mulligan and demands Josh be fired
- Brandon, Andy, and Jay sit down in the dining area and refuse to work
- Rob Mulligan calls Brandon back and says he's giving Josh a warning and begs Brandon to go back to work
- PH and a crowd of other supporters begin trickling into the store and occupying the dining area. A couple of them are sporting brown-bagged 40s of malt liquor.
- District manager Dylan arrives and orders the workers back to work. PH confronts him and demands Josh be fired.
- Rob calls Brandon back and says he's firing Josh and begs Brandon to go back to work. Brandon says they'll go back to work when Josh is out of the store with termination papers.
- Dylan fires Josh
- Dylan fires Brandon
- Cops arrive and everyone heads for the sidewalk

So, a mixed bag.

That night I hung out at Brandon's house with Brandon, Andy, PH, and several of their friends. I was generally supportive and tried to get them excited about the union. Then I went home, got drunk, and made a bunch of phone calls to coworkers and union friends. Eventually I left for a friend's house, where I got drunker and played poker until the early morning.

The following evening we had a meeting at Brandon's house. Thirteen adults and a couple of their kids attended, making it our largest committee meeting to date[51]. Half the JJ workers there, including lanky afroed David Beekie, had never been to a committee meeting before. Just about everybody was pumped at the turnout. The notable exception was myself, who considered the meeting one of the sloppiest we'd ever had.

In our eagerness to turn out as many of our coworkers as possible, we (and myself in particular) had invited coworkers with whom we hadn't done 1-on-1s and who were completely in the dark about the union campaign. So we spent the majority of the meeting fielding questions about the IWW, which in most cases Brandon and PH answered clumsily.

Once we passed the hour mark (more like the 2-hour mark, due to a late start), people became antsy for some course of action. So in ill-advised and hasty fashion, PH and Brandon decided they would circulate a petition for Brandon's reinstatement and we adjourned.

I drove some folks home, then went to the Bedlam and played a show with Terracide. I was so drunk while we were playing that I could barely stand.

The next day PH and Brandon went around to all the stores and approached workers across the counter asking them to sign a petition for Brandon's reinstatement. Stix, my best friend on the committee, got furious at PH for approaching him about the union in front of the owner, Mike Mulligan. PH got six of his coworkers at Block E to sign the petition but was furious that nobody at any of the other stores was organizing around the petition. Brandon filed an Unfair Labor Practices charge concerning his firing[52], and the Mulligans trespassed him from all their stores.

I spent the next week frantically trying to pick up the pieces.

I had excellent talks with many of my coworkers, including:

---

[51] Plus we met in a cramped living room, which as I mentioned back in footnote 19 makes a dozen feel like an army

[52] These typically take 2 months to 12 years for the board to decide

69

Shaggy: Ex-scumfuck Jesus punk who delivered sandwiches on a tall bike and once talked a guy out of mugging him by reasoning with him - "I helped your kid fix his bike! Look, just take the sandwich and come by the house when you've got the money." He of course told the mugger where he lived.

Geo: Tranny badass at Riverside who was struggling to stay off of heroin. I hung out with him and my other coworker Julia in a filthy apartment in Loring Park. Geo signed a union card.

Hunter: Young stoner with a pervy mustache who played in a rippin Minutemen-esque rock band.

TJ: Already mentioned in this narrative, but I'll add here that around this time he wanted to contribute to the campaign but even the 5 hours of corporate servitude a week he had cut back to made him nauseous.

Derrel: Smooth-talking Northsider whom I tried to teach how to play poker at the Dinkytowner bar.

David Beekie: Anti-zionist Jew and small forward. Also quite possibly the best Scrabble player I had ever met. I got the impression that he would contribute some much-needed discipline and accountability to the campaign.

Stix: In the Stix/PH feud, I unequivocally sided with Stix. Not necessarily because I thought he was right, but because I felt like I owed him. Stix had become one of my best friends, and I felt like he was the reason I was still involved in the union. I told Stix that I had his back, that if he quit I'd quit, and I begged him to stay involved with the campaign.

PH: I chewed PH out for approaching workers over the counter about Brandon's firing. How can you expect workers to feel anything but uneasy when a stranger tries to talk to them about a blacklisted worker in front of their boss? You're putting people in uncomfortable situations and making a target of yourself. It doesn't do us any good if you get fired too. Those and other admonitions that I more-or-less believed.

The Uptown work stoppage was the craziest and messiest action our campaign had ever attempted. One of our committee members lost his job, which scared the workers at Calhoun and made that store caustic towards our committee for months afterward. In the wake of the action, a sloppy and divided follow-up nearly tore our committee apart. PH became disheartened and didn't quit immediately but was clearly on his way out. Andy started getting screwed around for hours and lost faith in his coworkers, many of whom he considered tools for siding with management on Brandon's firing. He lost his enthusiasm for the quick service food industry and began looking for a train to hop.

But when the dust cleared a few weeks later, we had a functioning committee that was meeting regularly. We had picked up a few solid committee members in David, TJ, and Shaggy. Counting St. Louis Park JJ worker Rory, who had unwittingly walked in on the work stoppage and later attended a union meeting, we suddenly had union supporters at all 8 stores in the franchise. And for me personally, I had rediscovered my hope that we could accomplish something special at Jimmy John's.

A little hope can go a long way.

Chapter 22
Shitty Love Lives

April 10th, 2009

...Fuck, I didn't even know her name until the end of the night. But I put the moves on her, brought her home, ...[53]..., and here I am, Friday afternoon waiting to get stood up by Hunter and probably hang out with Brandon, feeling like a lousy idiotic worthless scumbag.

---

[53] Censored for squareness

I feel really dumb for not giving K------ a chance, given what a kind and sincere person she is and how fucking hot she is. But I think there's a good chance that I'm right and we're incompatible and it would not have worked out. I don't think she understands how fucked up I am and I don't think she'd be able to deal with me when I get depressed.

I also feel shitty about sleeping with P---- last night. I have absolutely no interest in her except sex. We didn't even trade phone numbers, didn't discuss hanging out again. Fine by me.

The union shit's getting hard again. Folks are afraid to talk to me. I'm working long hours and have no time for friends, etc. But fuck it, I'm going to keep fighting on that front, at least for now.

And you know what, fuck it, what's done is done. I've been really dumb about girls lately, but that doesn't mean I have to be dumb about C-------. I'm going to call her today.

I suppose I'd better go call Brandon.

A union organizer's greatest assets are time and passion. Time-consuming elements of your personal life — like say a girlfriend or kids — can act as barriers. Likewise, positives like a loving relationship or a hefty bank account can extinguish your agitational fire. What I'm trying to say is:

It helps to have a shitty love life.

My own organizing journal stands as a testament to the motivational power of an unfulfilling love life. What began as a just-the-facts-Jack account of my union organizing activities had by Spring 2009 become a drunken self-deprecating account of my rather typical and dissatisfying love life.

I pined over beautiful women, then got drunk and slept with their roommates instead. I'd act awkward around ladies I really liked and then end up in bed with people I hardly knew. I was the third set of genitalia in a jealousy-plagued open relationship. A queer lady I was way into warned me that we might be "sexually incompatible," and then I found out the rectal way that we were. Mostly I slept with women I thought I was into and then quickly broke it off with them when I decided I wasn't. And of course all the while I was still hung up on an old flame, which was probly the reason none of my relationships went anywhere in the first place.

And how did I deal with my relationship failures? I got drunk and poured my heart into organizing.

And how did I deal with my organizing failures? I got drunk and hit on the closest cutie.

One noteworthy example of this heated horny cycle from Spring 2008:

We have a crappy disheartening committee meeting. Later that week I find out that two of my best friends are quitting, and so is the new girl who I thought was going to make a great organizer. So I go out to the bar with my coworkers and I'm on fire. How much do you make in a week? What's your rent? Have you been getting the hours you need? Do you have any idea how much money the Mulligans are making off of us?

After the bar my good friend Leo tries to drop me off at home so he can try to get with our coworker K------, but I insist on coming with them to his brother's house. I throw down on bootleg after-hours beer and end up hammered and hanging out with some Mexican gangster guys and their girlfriends in an apartment by the Little Earth projects. I'm the only one who doesn't speak Spanish and I'm practically passed out the entire time, but whenever anyone references that fact I pop up spitting venom. Leo's friends are totally chill, whereas I'm a huge dick.

Afterwards K------ and I go back to my house and have sloppy drunk sex. In retrospect, I should have known her boyfriend would disapprove. Needless to say, that relationship doesn't go anywhere and I soon find myself at the bar again, trying to agitate my coworkers about our dismal day job.

Which is not to say that I often slept with coworkers. I entered the JJ campaign with a strict standard for myself — no sleeping with coworkers or union members. To me it was analogous to sleeping with a roommate or bandmate - the old "don't shit where you sleep" punk adage.

In practice, I've found the abstinence mentality to be entirely unrealistic. At JJs we never had a committee of 5 or more in which one of us wasn't sleeping with a coworker. And my record with roommates is far from clean. I would argue that sex is an inescapable symptom of any sizeable organization of humans[54].

The problem with sleeping with your co-conspirators is that when it doesn't work out[55], one of the parties will tend to drift away from the union. And in a majority-male organization like the organizing committee we were building at Jimmy John's, it was almost always the women who dropped out of the campaign and not the men.

I don't have any brilliant advice on that one. Solidarity's the best defense. Make sure that someone's partner isn't their only close friend on the committee. So that if and when they do break up, both parties will have friends encouraging them to stay involved. That's the theory, anyway.

Through organizing I had built intimate relationships with people from vastly disparate backgrounds, many of whom I considered very different from myself.

Well, shitty love lives and shitty jobs are the great equalizers. Once you get down to it, turns out that all people care about the same handful of issues. We all want to love, and we all want to be loved. If you can wrap your head around that one, then you can have a meaningful conversation with just about anyone.

---

[54] If an avowedly celibate institution like the priesthood is obsessed with sex, imagine the hormonal implications of joining a bridge club or a kickball team.

[55] It rarely does

74

Chapter 23
Gambling

A lifelong degenerate gambler, I've occasionally found ways to incorporate my vice into my organizing. So then, Spring and Summer 2009, as gambling exploits:

The Punch-Jimmy-In-The-Face Pool

April 26th, 2009
That Saturday fucking Jimmy John himself showed up at Dinkytown JJ. I had just been talking to Alex about my long-running idea of starting a punch-Jimmy-in-the-face pool, where a bunch of workers would pledge a certain amount of $, and the first guy to sock Jimmy would get the money. And then in walked the bastard.

Unlike at say Wendy's, at Jimmy John's there actually is a Jimmy John. He's a right-wing endangered-species-hunting misogynist fat man. At restaurants he insists on being served by attractive college girls. Once during my tenure at JJs, he visited the Skyway store downtown and demanded all the workers take their shirts off and called them "fags" when they didn't. He has oily tan rich person skin and wears a Jersey Shore chain and silk collared t-shirt.

I always thought it would be a fun idea to start a punch-Jimmy-in-the-face pool[56]. Sure you'd get fired, but what could be a better way to go? Especially if we could throw you some money to soften the judicial blow? And if we recorded the incident, what a viral video!

I finally got my chance to take a swing at Jimmy in April 2009, and I did nothing. He came into the store on a Saturday just as I was on my way out the back door with a delivery. My coworker recognized Jimmy from the giant picture of him that

---

[56] Not-so-fun would be criminal conspiracy charges against the union. Still, an idea.

75

hangs in every store. I noticed something was up and walked back into the store to meet him.

He wasn't as fat as I'd hoped - looked like some Italian mob douche. He had a trophy wife/mistress with him. He told us he was disappointed that the ceiling fan in our dining area wasn't fanning and that we weren't busy. He also told us that we owed him, because his brand was the reason we had jobs.

I wish I would have told him that he owed us, because we busted our asses to make him hundreds of millions of dollars while we struggled to break even every month. Or punched him in the face. I didn't do either. All I can say is that I refused to shake his hand and was salty about staffing.

I stand by my opinion. Somebody needs to punch that motherfucker in the face.

Powerball Pool

August 13th, 2009

Did the powerball pool again yesterday. What a brilliant idea. I'm really patting myself on the back for that one. This week Nick, Altan, Brenda, TJ, Stix, Davis, and myself all threw in $3. I biked to the Grease Pit, 9th St., and Calhoun after work to collect money and agitate. We didn't win, sadly. $196 million jackpot too.

In Summer 2009 our organizing committee was looking stronger than ever. We had picked up a few fresh faces, notably:

Lita Shore: Recent high school graduate who worked at the Franklin-Nicollet store. A petite lady with gorgeous brown eyes, Lita had some edge to her and fit right in talking trash with her burlier streetwise coworkers.

Ayo: An old friend of Lita's, Ayo had just started at the 9th St. store downtown. Also a recent high school graduate, he had an afro and mismatched socks and was determined to

76

establish himself as the craziest motherfucker on two wheels in Minneapolis.

Davis Ritzema: New hire at the Uptown store. Davis had previously had a disappointing experience salting[57] with a UNITE-HERE hotel campaign. He also had too many jobs and a large hammer and sickle tattoo on his ass.

The committee was growing, and we were getting more serious. I was so pleased with the direction of the campaign that in a moment of inspiration I started a Powerball pool.

We would spend our whole shift on lottery day talking about our post-jackpot lives. We always began with a whirlwind vacation of the world. Everybody had to pick a country.

After that you got into what you would do with millions of dollars. I would buy a bunch of muscle and consolidate power over the soda machines in South Minneapolis. I would hire 5 Texans with conceal-and-carry permits to follow me around in cowboy regalia performing a Riverdance. Hundreds of pounds of smoked salmon. Vanilla Ice. These and other items I would buy.

We also talked about our debts, our families, our home-owning aspirations. Basically what we would do if we weren't working for poverty wages at Jimmy John's.

There's a stereotype of fast food and food service in general as being full of students who don't really need money. First of all, I've worked at 7 pizza places and 10 Jimmy Johns', and I've never seen a store that was majority students.

But more importantly, nobody works at Jimmy John's for fun. They work there because they need the money, for one reason or another. Students, dropouts, felons, corporate kissasses – everybody works there because they need the paycheck. I've worked with students who were supporting their parents with their JJ checks, and I've worked with homeless

---

[57] In the AFL-CIO world, "salting" means getting a job at a workplace where a union has an ongoing organizing campaign and reporting on your coworkers to union staffers.

guys who spent their meager paychecks on food and drink. Don't ever doubt that we need the money.

The Powerball pool was a fun means of bringing out everybody's reasons for needing the money. It also brought attention to our miserably low wages. And in the back of my mind, I thought we had a pretty good chance of winning the jackpot[58].

Poker Nights

July 28th, 2009

Sunday was poker night at my house, not too successful. David and Lita were out of their league. One good thing that came out of it was Mojo talked about his experience with union busters at the Lagoon Theater. Lita was the last one to leave and I felt like we had an awkward goodbye.

Besides my awful Sunday shift at Riverside, work's been decent but exhausting. Today was particularly brutal. My legs are shot.

A couple things I'd like to mention-

1. Our meetings are really well-organized these days. We start on time, have a facilitator, take notes and e-mail them to a list-serve, stick to an agenda, have a basic agenda outline for every meeting. There's still a little drinking that goes on.

2. I feel like a bunch of different worlds are colliding for me these days, and it all comes back to JJs. Stix is going to punk shows and picking up punk girls. David and Lita are hanging out with my roommates and poker buddies. One of the RNC 8 is getting a job at JJs. All in all I think that's really good. I want to go crazy with JJ stuff this fall, and the time for keeping my JJ activities under wraps is almost over.

A common wobbly criticism of anarchist/activist projects is that they are just "activists organizing activists."

---

[58] Degenerate gambler, mind you

Part of the reason I believed in the potential of union organizing was that I was working with all kinds of people from all kinds of backgrounds. I'll always be a punk to some extent, but by the age of 25 I'd come to believe that punk is a ghetto and will never be the driving force in any significant political movement.

When I started organizing at Jimmy John's I made a concerted effort to keep my punk life separate from my work life. I didn't flyer at the shops for shows my band played, I never played punk music on the store stereos, and I didn't invite my coworkers to punk parties.

Initially I was trying to keep the campaign a secret. I didn't want everyone in the music scene to know that we were organizing at Jimmy John's. By Summer 2009 we had completely failed in that department and pretty much everyone knew about the campaign[59].

I also didn't want to intimidate my coworkers by taking them to parties full of drunk black-clad foul-mouthed punks who all knew each other and were wary of norms[60]. I felt that if the punk scene became associated with the union, then we would push non-punks away and our committee would become a cliquey dirty white minority of the JJs workforce.

In Summer 2009 I started to change my tune.

Lita proposed to the committee that we establish a social night for union members outside of organized meetings. She wanted to do a weekly low-stakes poker night where we could relax and drink beers and get to know each other better. Being the degenerate gambler that I am, I jumped at that idea and offered to host poker nights at my house.

Poker night had a short run of two months, but it significantly altered my approach to creating union culture. I invited poker buddies of mine who didn't work at JJs, and it was not the complete disaster I feared. I started inviting

---

[59] How did the bosses not find out? Heads up their asses, I expect.
[60] Punk definition of "norm": Person who is not drunk black-clad and foul-mouthed.

coworkers to punk shows we had in our basement, and that was nothing but fun either.

Besides poker nights and punk shows, committee members also started going in groups to bar shows that Davis's psychedelic rock band Dante The Lobster played. We went to bike messenger keg parties and derbied bikes[61] in living rooms with Stix and Ayo's friends.

I can't speak for other jobs, but at JJs our collective partying endeavors did not make our coworkers think of us as cliquey weirdos. Instead, we became cooler[62]. Our coworkers actually wanted to come to our parties and shows. And in those twilight hours on sticky beer-covered dance floors we passed out union cards and argued passionately for the power of solidarity.

It was starting to feel like a union.

Chapter 24
A Visit To The Labor Board Office

September 9th, 2009

After practice I went down to the labor board office with Lita, David, TJ, and Max. I was fucking filthy, covered in engine grease and whatnot. I'm afraid I did most of the talking, asked this lawyer a bunch of questions. All the news was good. We're looking at 55 days between filing and an election, 42 days if we're lucky. That's the bad news, but we knew that.

After that Lita took TJ and I to the river where we finished a crossword, drank beers, and ate pork rinds. Then TJ and I put up a flyer for the race at Dinkytown and scoped out the race endpoint to find a good route.

---

[61] It's like NASCAR except in a living room on bicycles and the object is to knock everyone off their bikes. Maybe it's more like jousting. Somewhere between NASCAR and jousting. On bicycles.

[62] Which is not to say we weren't cool already. I was, you know, in a band.

As Summer turned to Fall our committee continued to grow, a notable new addition being:

Max Spektor: Pianist/punk facing bogus "conspiracy to commit terrorism" charges in connection with the 2008 RNC. Fearless and clever, Max in no time at all was making some of the best jokes in the committee.

We finally had 10 solid committee members, plus another 25 union supporters who had signed authorization cards. We decided it was time for an all-out push to file for a union election. Course, none of us had any experience in union elections, so we took a road trip to the labor board office downtown and had a Q & A with a hearing officer. He seemed fairly amused – he normally dealt with lawyers, not young filthy service industry workers.

A brief summary of the union election process:

- First, the union must demonstrate a "showing of interest" – 30% of the proposed bargaining unit must sign some sort of petition saying they want union representation.
- Next, the union and the company have to agree on an election date, bargaining unit, and polling places/times. If the union and the company can't reach an election agreement, then the labor board will hold a hearing and you'll have your election in 55 days.
- Eligible voters in an election are workers in the bargaining unit who received a paycheck the pay period before you filed your petition.
- A majority of the votes cast reject the union and you lose. You know, usually.
- A bunch of other legalistic tedium, but that's the guts of the operation.

Our biggest fears were:

1. The company would demand and win an unreasonable bargaining unit, say all the JJs in Minnesota. Something along those lines had happened to an IWW election at a Starbucks in NYC. The hearing officer reassured us that due to the franchise structure of JJs (Mike Mulligan signed my paychecks, not Jimmy John), we need not worry about this.
2. The company would take us to a hearing over the bargaining unit then appeal the decision of the hearing, dragging out the election process. The hearing officer told us that this was also unlikely. Probably.

Meanwhile Stix had organized a 2nd Jimmy John's bike race, and this one was much more successful than the first. This time 16 workers ran the race and a dozen more helped at stops.

Before it started, Stix announced that the IWW had paid for the keg at the after party. The thinking – fuck it, this shit's not gonna be a secret much longer anyway. We had set a deadline for filing the election – Halloween.

As I sprinted across the city, sweating balls with my smoker's lungs screaming at me, part of me couldn't wait for the

THE SAMMICH RACE:
An Age Old tradition
5¢
FREE BEER
FOR JJ eMPLoYeeS
JiMMY Bike RacE !
StarT: Eliot Park
3 PM SHARP
Finish: 3½ Gramercy
Northside
+ PARTY AFTER
6 PM TiL LATE
SUN. 9/6

election to be over and done with so I could move on with my life. I was 2 years past burnt out on organizing, and I had decided that after the election I was leaving JJs one way or another.

There was another part of me, though, that was having the time of my life. I was high on adrenaline with a belly full of beer at a bike race after party. After 2 ½ years of hard work and heartbreak, we were finally about to hold the largest union election in the history of American fast food. A light at the end of the tunnel. Or so it seemed.

Chapter 25
Working Hurt

November 3rd, 2009

Let's see, got nailed by a car a few weeks ago, 10/19/09. I know that cause since then I've been talking to insurance people and lawyers and the stupid college girl who hit me and broke my collarbone. She wants $850 for the damage my body did to her bumper. Fucking bullshit.

My bike is back to rideable but still jenky as hell. The fork is too long, chain ring's bent. I've been borrowing Laila's grandma baskets and rack the past couple weeks cause I can't wear my bag. Oh, and I've been delivering with a broken collarbone for a week and a half.

I'm totally broke, short on rent till I get my measly paycheck on the 6th. I also don't have money to buy a new alternator.

My collarbone has healed enough that I can lift my arm to write again. But I'm still in pretty rough shape physically. Besides my shoulder, my back, my neck, and my legs all kill.

I've been getting paranoid that I have a tumor in my chest, but I think that's just paranoia. I probably should go get checked out anyway. My chest has been hurting.

I'm generally just in rough shape. My body hurts, I feel like shit about the campaign (which has more or less stalled), I feel like shit about my love life, and I really have nothing else going on. I'm slacking at everything, watching sports and playing chess and getting drunk.

Oh, and I hate hate hate my job.

It does feel good to be writing again though. Hopefully I'll have better news in the future.

One night I was biking home from work through an unlit stretch of 20th Ave South when I hit a nasty pothole. I flew over my handlebars and crumpled into the pavement. Then, slowly, I peeled myself off the street, adjusted my headset, and biked home. I spent that night glued to the couch, drinking whiskey and watching Battlestar Gallactica. The next day I popped a couple Ibuprofen and biked to work.

About a week later I started having trouble breathing. I couldn't take deep breaths. I didn't know if it was anxiety or emphysema or what, so I went to the clinic. The diagnosis – two broken ribs and a broken sternum. The internal swelling was pushing against my lungs so that they couldn't fully inflate.

At Jimmy John's I became accustomed to working in pain. Broken ribs I didn't even bother getting checked - I assumed they'd just prescribe me Ibuprofen. I couldn't afford to miss work, so I didn't, sometimes going to ridiculous lengths to deliver my sandwiches.

The most dangerous condition I ever delivered in was after I broke my collarbone. It happened at work so I qualified for Worker's Comp, but I couldn't afford to lose my tips, so I went back to work before I could lift my arm above my waist. I put baskets on my bike, since I couldn't wear a bag while my collarbone healed. The baskets and rack nearly doubled the weight of my bike, which made work that much more difficult.

For weeks I biked with one arm and those heavy-ass baskets, navigating around Minneapolis's icy streets in below-zero wind chills to make my measly tips.

I was certainly not the first or last JJ worker to work with broken bones. Stix in fact worked with the exact same injury – a broken collarbone – on two occasions.

More common than working through pain was working through sickness. I have a lifetime's worth of horror stories on that one too. Like David's coworker at the Skyway store leaving the hospital to work her lunch shift and then returning to the hospital after work, where she was inpatient. Or Micah Barley being required to stay and find his own replacement while his lung collapsed.

If you're a downtown suit making six figures and have to miss a day of work, you could be out $1,000. If you work at Jimmy John's and have to miss a day of work, you could be out $40. Intuitively you'd think that the worker who stands to lose more money would be more likely to work hurt or sick. You'd be wrong.

Jimmy John's is not special in this regard. I would argue that low wage workers are always more likely to work through pain and sickness than their higher paid counterparts. It's not so much the dollar amount that matters, it's why you need the money. $20 towards rent is always more valuable than $1,000 towards savings.

In the service industry, working sick is the norm. I once talked to a deathly ill cook at the CC Club in Uptown who told me he hadn't taken a sick day in 10 years.

The JJ campaign to me was always about more than just our immediate circumstances. We were organizing in a completely unorganized industry where workers had no benefits and were accustomed to working conditions that would horrify 9 to 5 white collar types. I thought that if we could improve life at our job, we'd inspire workers in similar positions to organize and improve their own jobs.

But before we reached that point, there was pain.

Chapter 26
War Council

November 17th, 2009

Oh, last Wednesday there was a failed "War Council" meeting at Stix's. I watched 3 movies and had an awkward end of the night hanging out with Stix and Lita.

Tomorrow I'm meeting with Lita, Nate White, Ayo, and Forman. And skipping the War Council meeting.

November 19th, 2009

Then we went to the post-"war council" hangout at Stix's. The war council meeting was apparently just Stix and Beekie, but Stix didn't seem too upset about it.

Our Halloween deadline for going public came and went, and we did not reach our goal of getting a majority of workers to sign authorization cards. We didn't even come close really – about 40 workers short. So we didn't file for an election, and we didn't go public as a union.

Instead, we did what everybody does when faced with missed deadlines – we pushed the deadline back. In committee meetings I spoke against having a deadline at all, but I was in the minority. The position I'd held for years was that I didn't want to go public without a majority of workers. No deadline could change that. But I was voted down, which in a sense actually felt good, because it meant that I was no longer the sole driving force of the campaign.

So, hypothetically we were still going public any day. Given that, Stix wanted to strike a subcommittee called the "War Council" that would be responsible for creating a detailed timeline of public actions the union would carry out after we announced ourselves to the world. The "War Council" would predict the company backlash and have prepared responses – the defensive strategy. It would also prepare an offensive strategy of actions geared around our demands.

I found the whole idea silly. Why worry about what we'd do when we went public if we couldn't even organize enough support to go public? I wanted the focus of our organizing committee to be on 1-on-1 meetings and job actions around grievances.

"War Council" also felt undemocratic to me. How could we preplan actions? If the fallout from the Uptown work stoppage had taught me anything it was that workers won't participate in job actions if they don't participate in their planning. You don't tell workers to go on strike – you tell them to plan their own strike.

But I was glad that Stix was participating in the union, so in a lapse of judgment I decided to passively let "War Council" do its own thing and fizzle out without my involvement, meanwhile ridiculing it in my notebook by always writing it in quotation marks. In retrospect – probably one of my bigger missteps in the entire campaign[63].

War Council began meeting on Wednesdays at Stix's house and by all accounts was a complete failure. Attendance hovered between 0 and 3. Besides Stix, David Beekie was the only committed participant. David tried to institute agendas and organize actual meetings, but every meeting eventually denigrated into a booze and pot fest where most of the folks hanging out didn't even work at Jimmy John's and the conversation centered more around pop culture than work. An echo of the earlier failures of the campaign.

Meanwhile I was holding 1-on-1's with my new coworkers and committee members, notably:

April: A queer punk partier, April was prone to all kinds of scandal and scene drama. A righteous battle-tested lady, she was caring and supportive towards people she liked but vicious towards assholes and creeps. And she was now my coworker at the Riverside store!

Erik Forman: The intrepid Starbucks organizer had somehow gotten hired into the brand new JJs at the West End in St. Louis Park[64]! He was only committing to working 10 hours a week, but nevertheless he did his first 1-on-1 with a coworker before his first shift!

Despite the new additions to our committee, morale within the campaign began to plummet as winter approached.

War Council was discontinued after nobody showed up to a meeting. Stix became completely disheartened and left the organizing committee, never to return. I felt like I had set him up for failure, allowing him to go through with a project I considered doomed all along instead of working with him to make it successful.

---

[63] The passive scorn, not the quotation marks themselves
[64] The 9th store in our franchise, opened in late 2009.

87

But besides Stix dropping out of the union, our failure to achieve majority support demoralized everybody. Just months earlier we had felt so close, but now with the opening of yet another store we realized how truly far away we were. Even our militant member TJ told me that he now felt like we would not be able to "unionize" Jimmy John's, but that we could still accomplish some things. I felt like we were right back where we had been a year earlier, when Arnaldas had asked me if it was even worth trying.

Chapter 27
Black Eyes

Easter Sunday April 12th, 2009
But we left separately and I ended up getting in a fight with some guy. I was all keyed up and he pushed my Chrome button, making my messenger bag fall off as I was walking past him. I talked a bunch of shit, forced him into the bathroom (?), headbutted him, got headbutted back. Dude told me he was going to get his gun out of his back pocket and I said, "You can't!" Later, as my friends were dragging me outside, I was like, "Go get your gun, motherfucker!" So that's that.

Now I have a killer headache and I'm wondering if writing group is on for today.

August 5th, 2009
Friday night I got in a fight with Dan Parkinson. I asked him if he was getting into fascism, which is what I'd been hearing. He's not. He got mad and started preaching all this nihilistic bullshit at me, notably that organizing at JJ is a waste of time. I followed him upstairs, swung at him and missed, then he gave me a black eye. Then metal Luke threw me into a couple walls as I tried to get at Dan. Someone else too, can't remember.

Then I went to the Bedlam, talked to Savannah. Then to Medusa, set up a 1-on-1 with Jonathon Kennedy. We met up

Saturday at the Wienery. He signed a card and said he's coming to the meeting Thursday.

August 27th, 2009

I got the shit kicked out of me two Friday's ago after a hip hop show at the Shit Biscuit. I had left to give Nick a ride home (drove really drunk, by the way) and came back at like 4:30am. Confronted 4 crusties on the sidewalk, told them they had to leave, got my ass rocked, acoustic guitar smashed over the head, etc.

Then I was laid up for a few days, got hooked on Battlestar Gallactica. TJ came over that Saturday and made BLTs and watched BSG with me. That was really cool.

December 15th, 2009

Well, I've been under a lot of stress lately.

Big news was I got in a fight at Hard Times 2 Mondays ago, collected my third black eye of 2009. I was drinking at Palmers with Stix, having a really good time. He bought me a shot of Rumplemints, which is I think what did me in.

I don't even remember Round 1 of the fight. Blacked out in front of Hard Times. Came in with a bloody face. Somehow pointed out the guy to Stix, who ran outside and tackled him. I jumped on top of him and started pounding on dude's head. Johnny ended up driving me home.

That turned into a really shitty week at work. I'm so goddamn broke I couldn't afford to take a week off of work, so I ended up biking with one eye all week in the nastiest of nasty conditions. Below zero temps, streets full of snow and ice, winds gusting to 40 mph. Fuck that sucked. But I made it through it and now my eye is open again.

For reasons not entirely clear to me, I got in several fights in 2009. Before I headbutted graffiti guy Ian I had not been in a fight in five years.

On New Year's 2010 I made a resolution to not collect any more black eyes.

Days later, after a party at my house, I woke up to shouting. My roommate and fellow union member April was telling some nameless faceless entity to leave. I got out of bed, went upstairs to the the third floor, threw the anonymous man down the stairs.

On the second floor landing we had an unfriendly debate. I grabbed his wrists so that he could not punch me in the eye, as per my New Year's resolution. After a crowd had gathered and I deemed it safe to separate, I released the wrists. And wouldn't you know it, no sooner had I released the wrists then a fist came flying from around the head of one of my peacemaking roommates, striking me below the eye.

The next day my eye was tender but did not turn black. Since then I have not been in a fist fight.

Some conclusions I drew from my year of fisticuffs:

1. Fists have a natural tendency to find my eyes. I never once got a bloody nose, but whenever somebody threw a fist at me it found my eyes. I often have received compliments on my eyes and consider them my best feature. Cuts both ways, apparently.
2. Do not pick fights with groups of people. Groups by definition have numerical superiority.
3. Alcohol does not make you faster, stronger, or smarter. Quite the opposite.
4. I would never pick a fight I knew I could win.

Chapter 28
Harassment

January 5th, 2010

Then April and I went to Palmers and talked more and now I'm thinking that if April can't get hired in at Calhoun we should pursue the sexual harassment angle. Mike's been saying fucked up shit at work for a long time (talking about raping girls till they bleed, saying he's going to keep hiring girls till he gets laid, etc.) , and he has a history of domestic abuse (his ex left him for putting her in the hospital on multiple occasions). I also think he's trying to get with Emily, the new hire.

At Dinkytown we had a night manager named Jason.

When Jason was alone working with women he was an asshole. He called our coworker Angela fat and kept telling her not to be a bitch. He made uncomfortable sex jokes and mimicked female orgasms. Multiple women quit or refused to work nights because of his behavior.

Jason was also a bigoted white guy. He called Arizona a "breeding ground for Mexicans." On two occasions he fired black coworkers of ours under bogus pretexts like telling them they weren't scheduled and then firing them for missing their shift.

Anyway, we hated him.

In Fall 2009 TJ started organizing around a petition to demand that our bosses the Mulligans fire Jason. The petition described his behavior in graphic detail. TJ spoke with all our coworkers and circulated the petition in the store. When I signed it I was the 10th signature.

Before we submitted the petition we had a meeting of Dinkytown JJ workers about how we'd do it. This, by the way, is how you should organize all job actions. Have a separate meeting about the action outside of your regular business meetings. The actions we did without their own meeting were never as successful.

After we submitted the petition, Jason had a closed-door meeting with his higher-ups and was warned but not fired. Then he stopped harassing his employees. Since the problem appeared solved, the majority opinion in the shop was to drop the issue, which we did. Jason was later fired for something unrelated.

This is how workers should deal with sexual harassment: collective direct action.

Later in 2009 the union ran into a skeezier fucker, and this time we dealt with it poorly.

Mike J. had become the general manager of the Riverside store and immediately begun hiring exclusively young girls.

Every day at work Mike would make raunchy sex jokes – preteen, anal, rape – take your pick. He "jokingly" humped female employees against countertops. He perused sex worker advertisements on the office computer. He even read the Twilight books.

I found all this incredibly creepy, but none of it was directed at me and my coworkers all said they didn't feel threatened. They just thought he was being weird. So I did nothing.

One day at work Mike was talking about how he was going to keep hiring young girls until he got laid. April called him out for it and they got into a big argument. Shortly thereafter he cut her hours. Then after Christmas he tried to fire the both of us.

I got a call from Max telling me he'd seen the new holiday season schedule and I wasn't on it. I immediately drove down to the store and met up with Max, then we went inside and confronted Mike together. Luckily we'd caught him off guard.

Mike said that he was adding drivers to the shifts I was working, and since I didn't want more drivers on my shifts, he hadn't scheduled me. I said yeah, but I still need a job. We argued for several minutes, then when I had lost hope and was sure I was fired, Max convinced Mike to come in the back of the store with us and look at the new schedule. We found a couple 3-hour evening shifts that were still open and Mike, looking defeated, wrote me in for them.

I'd lost all my hours, but I wasn't fired. I subsequently covered a bunch of shifts around the franchise until I could get more hours at Dinkytown.

April was not so lucky.

On my way home from Max saving my job, it occurred to me that April wasn't on the schedule either. So I called her and told her.

Instead of confronting Mike with a group, April called him and talked to him 1-on-1. He said he'd meet with her on Monday, giving him the weekend to get his story straight. Monday morning she met with him and he fired her. His stated reason was that she had "gotten upset about getting her hours cut" and "stayed upset too long."

With April and me out of the store, Mike went ahead with his fucked up sexual vision for the Riverside JJs. I heard about workers getting pissed when he gave all the good shifts to a college freshman he was dating. Then after they broke up he hired another young girl and started fucking her. Turned out he hadn't been joking, and that had been his plan all along.

Mike J. would eventually get fired for sexual harassment — forcing a female employee to look at internet porn, specifically — but it would be due to the efforts of a different group of workers, long after I had been exiled from the store.

I do not mean to imply that most managers are creeps and bigots. Usually they are not. But this is a case where Murphy's Law applies — given enough managers, if there's little or no penalty for sexual harassment and racial discrimination, some manager is going to harass and discriminate.

Ideally, companies should have and enforce harassment/discrimination policies. Jason and Mike J.'s behavior should never have been tolerated.

In reality, it's on workers to enforce these policies. The morale drop within our committee towards the end of 2009 had led to a falloff in organizing. We weren't doing 1-on-1s, and as a result we were too disorganized to deal with Mike J. April and I allowed ourselves to get drawn into isolated screaming matches with him. He fired her, and eventually he banned me from ever working at Riverside.

*

2010

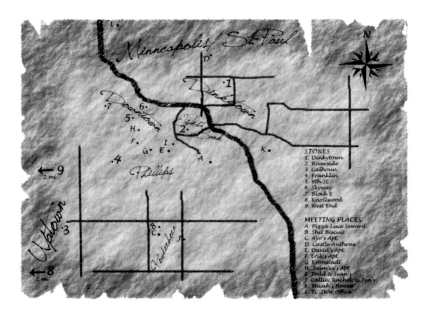

Minneapolis / St. Paul

Dinkytown

Cedar Riverside

Downtown

Phillips

Uptown

← 9
2 mi

3

← 8
2 mi

Franklin

Riverside

N

STORES
1. Dinkytown
2. Riverside
3. Calhoun
4. Franklin
5. 9th St
6. Skyway
7. Block E
8. Knollwood
9. West End

MEETING PLACES
A. Pizza Luce Seward
B. Shit Biscuit
C. Ajo's Apt.
D. Castle Anthrax
E. David's Apt
F. Erik's Apt.
G. Kronstadt
H. Jaimee's Apt
I. Todd & Sean's
J. Callie, Rachel & Jen's
K. Micah's House
L. TC IWW Office

January 31ˢᵗ, 2010

I'm not really sure how to move forward. My intent is to focus on the contact list and getting cards signed. It seems like it all comes back to 1-on-1s, always, it's just a matter of getting people pumped up to do them. Myself included of course.

I think I'm going to quit on Mayday, and I would really like it if we filed before that. I suppose I could just cut back to one night a week or something instead of quitting – I'm flexible on that, but I'm out after Mayday.

April 27ᵗʰ, 2010

Otherwise I pretty much feel like shit. Life has ceased to be fulfilling for me – I need a new project or something. Maybe I'm just getting old, I don't know. I feel like my crappy-ass job has completely consumed me and drained me of any motivation to do anything I actually enjoy. That shit sucks. I have to get out of this fucking campaign. I promised myself I'd quit on Mayday, but I'm not going to. Fucking union. Well I'm quitting after this fucking election goddamnit.

Chapter 29
Burnout

The first union meeting is like your first underground punk show. It's thrilling, scary, new. I could get fired! I might have to do public speaking! These guys are all commies! Etc.

Inevitably there's a downswing in the campaign. Somebody quits. Somebody breaks up with their partner and the facebook drama is all too much. Or maybe it's just really fucking cold outside. You fail to follow through on your plans, the committee stops meeting, and it's all very sad.

But then it warms up and you meet that awesome new coworker and it's time to start making grand plans again! So you do your 1-on-1s, set up a meeting, and before you know it you have a bona fide organizing committee that's bound to bring the bosses to their knees with brilliantly brazen direct action and solidarity unionism!

Inevitably there's a downswing in the campaign. Somebody quits, somebody breaks up with their partner...

Okay, now repeat that cycle about 8 times over 3 years and that's where I was with the Jimmy John's campaign entering 2010.

I had spoken to literally hundreds of coworkers about working conditions at JJs. I had become intimate friends with dozens of righteous people who had joined the committee. I had stood side by side with union members and told off bosses for bullshit firings and harassment.

Problem was, hardly any of these people still worked there. Except of course the bosses. And most of the friends I had made disappeared from my life as soon as they left the job. I had a high turnover personal life.

I had also delivered about 20,000 sandwiches and prepared somewhere around 100,000 sandwiches. Hundreds of times I had signed my initials on those ridiculous punch sheets to record my dishwashing activities. Thousands of times I had scooped mayo out of a bin and quickly spread it over french bread, careful not to miss the corners[65].

And then there were all the tired arguments.

I had worked at 7 different pizza places and nowhere had I dealt with management that constantly tweaked staffing like they did at Jimmy John's. Which in and of itself sucked, but what drove me crazy even more was arguing with my coworkers over and over again about the same old shit.

I had a coworker Altan at Dinkytown who was always defending overstaffing on the basis that it would lead to increased sales so eventually we'd have more deliveries. Again and again I'd explain to him that increased sales does not mean increased tips. The best money I ever made at Jimmy John's was working understaffed lunch shifts at Riverside, the slowest store in the franchise for deliveries[66].

---

[65] As the corporate slogan goes – Never a Dry Bite!

[66] I wrote a longer explanation of this phenomenon and then deleted it because it was boring. Apply logic if interested. The staffing equation also holds true for waitresses, bartenders, and cab drivers.

And finally all the union arguments, which after you hear them a few hundred times sound simple to you but somehow baffle others. Examples:

It's dishonest to meet behind your manager's back. You should talk to them 1-on-1 if you have grievances.

Organizing a union at Jimmy John's is silly because nobody cares about their job there anyway.

You're a white guy, so you're not being exploited.

At a certain point for me these arguments became old hat. I stopped having good faith conversations and started yelling. It's obvious damnit!

My friend and organizing mentor Nate once warned me that burnout was inevitable. Even paid staff organizers of mainstream unions get burnt out and rarely make careers out of it. The trick was allowing organizers to step back but stay involved in the union so they could return to fight another day.

I myself was years past burnt out. I had burnt out and quit, but somehow a year and a half later I was still working at Jimmy John's and agitating my coworkers. My only explanation for how I beat the burnout bug for so long:

I hated losing.

Fast food in the United States is by all accounts unorganizable. I had bet 3 years of my life that this was not true. As much as I hated my job and was tired of arguing, I still wanted to win. So I stuck around.

In February 2010, after another dismal Minneapolis January, the JJ organizing committee started meeting again. We had two consecutive meetings / pizza parties at Pizza Luce in Seward[67], and after that we returned to rotating between committee members' houses.

Game on.

---

[67] South Minneapolis neighborhood known for its aging hippie population

Chapter 30
Managers

April 18th, 2010

So last night Emily and I met up with J--- at Palmers and discussed the union. Big news:

The last manager meeting Krysta the GM at Skyway was apparently going wild warning Mike Mulligan and Rob about the union drive. J--- also implied that Mike Mulligan had approached corporate JJ about the union. And that they think the campaign is centered or at least strongest at the Dinkytown store. J--- said that Mike Mulligan recognized our legal right to organize but wanted us to meet with him to discuss our grievances rather than form a union.

Emily was disappointed that J--- wasn't more supportive and that he was demeaning about it. "Our little union," etc. He wanted to come to a meeting and we told him he couldn't.

He also offered to get us P & L (Profit and Loss) reports for every store in the franchise if he could come to a meeting.

There's a wobbly maxim that goes something like this: Without supervisors, the revolution would already have happened.

In food service, supervisors are called managers, and they come in all shapes and sizes. District managers, general managers, assistant managers, shift managers. Workaholics, lazy assholes, goofy weirdos, humorless asskissers. During my time at JJs I worked for over 100 managers spanning a pretty wide range of human personalities. Their one common characteristic: they all had a job to do, and that job was keeping workers in line.

In anti-union campaigns, union busters organize managers into the anti-union army[68]. They do this through coercion, deceit, and sometimes bribery. Managers have the

---

[68] I recommend Confessions of a Union Buster by Martin J. Levitt for a soul-crushing depiction of the union busting industry. Or just keep reading.

option of fighting the union or losing their job. In almost all cases they do what they're told. As a union organizer, I knew this.

But there's a gray area in restaurants that poses a challenge for organizing — in many cases your manager doesn't feel like a boss to you.

At Jimmy John's we worked side by side with our managers, and our managers did the same work that we did. Most of our working conditions were not dictated by general managers. They couldn't give us time and a half on holidays, or health insurance, or a decent wage. The majority of our demands could only be granted by franchise ownership or corporate JJs.

Occasionally you'd have that asshole manager who was sexually harassing people or screwing you around on hours, but in most cases I got along fine with my managers and in some cases became close friends with them.

I also sympathized with their working conditions. I remember cashing paychecks for two different assistant managers of mine. The checks were for the same shocking amount: $698. Assistant managers at Dinkytown worked 55 hours a week at a minimum, so that was take home pay for 2 weeks at a rate of $698 / 110 = $6.35 an hour, less than minimum wage[69].

But at the end of the day they were still supervisors, and they still had authority over us.

I can't tell you how many times somebody told me, upon my discussing the union with them for the first time, that I "should talk to Manager X, cause they hate JJs and are in a better position to help.[70]" For many people that's their gut reaction. If there's a problem, appeal to an authority figure for help.

---

[69] Managers in food and retail are often classified as salaried employees as a means of bypassing overtime regulations. It's quite the racket.

[70] Well, I could ballpark it. Let's say 50 times.

We're raised to believe in authority. When faced with crisis, call your mom. Tell a teacher. Get a lawyer. Vote Democrat. Pray.

In a union we teach people not to look up for help, but to instead look to the side. The ultimate goal of a union is not necessarily to get people raises, it's to empower people by showing them that together we have power. For this reason more than any other, managers cannot join the union.

Still, by 2010 I had two close friends who had become general managers of JJ stores in our franchise. I also had assistant manager and shift manager friends. All of them were well aware of the union campaign.

As winter turned to Spring our committee started once again kicking ass[71]. As a result of our ass-kicking we picked up several new committee members, notably:

Emily Przski – One of my all time favorite coworkers, and a rare lady bike delivery driver. I would vote her most likely to throw a sandwich across the store for no goddamn good reason.

Jared Ingebretz: Soft-spoken activist type, he became involved in the committee and immediately began working on badass imagery for the union, like this:

---

[71] And by that I mean conducting 1-on-1s with our coworkers. 1-on1's, 1-on-1's, 1-on-1's.

100

In April, the committee voted after much discussion to allow Emily and I to meet with one of our managers and discuss the union. We were both good friends with him and wanted to see if he would act as a pipeline for the union into management discussions. We weren't going to tell him anything about our plans or who was involved until he contributed to the union effort in such a way that would put his job at risk, say by giving us sensitive company documents.

We went barhopping around the West Bank and got all kinds of drunk. The union discussions were more or less a bust. J--- was alternately dismissive of the union and then would come back and tell us how much he much dirt he could dig up for us.

The highlights of the night for me:
1. I pegged 20 in one hand of cribbage[72]
2. J--- told us that in a recent manager meeting one of the GMs had been raving wild to the owners about the union campaign.

For the first time we knew that the owners were aware of the union effort. It was only a matter of time before they started targeting key organizers and trying to fire us. All the more reason to get our asses in gear.

Chapter 31
"The Scene"

May 12th, 2010
In scene news the crusty punx had a meeting on kicking K----- out of the scene. B------ woke up with K----- in her bed and his hand down her pants. So the crusties have finally turned on the fucker. Sounds like Manda organized the meeting. Hammer was there, so was Max, so was Rudolfo, probly a lot of other people I know. I had to work. Story of my fucking life.

---

[72] 3 aces, 4 aces, plus a 31

Hm, what else. Terracide played a pretty fun show at the Rathole Saturday. I dropped in on their new half-pipe. Hung out a lot longer than I thought I would. Decent people, just too much drugs and macho bullshit. I think some of those kids are still on trying to be apolitical and talk shit about activism, but I could give a fuck. I don't have much in common with activists myself these days, if I ever did.

I once had a charismatic punk-as-fuck roommate. We drank many beers together and became good friends. Then my roommates and I kicked him out of our house for beating his girlfriend and dealing cocaine to 15-year-olds.

In the following years several women accused him of raping them, and he became unpopular in Minneapolis. But he still had a tight circle of friends amongst the crusty punks. They defended him and played music with him and bought coke from him.

In 2010 he finally assaulted the wrong woman, and his friends turned against him. The punks organized meetings on how to kick him out of the scene, and then they kicked him out of the scene. It was one of those rare moments where folks from all different cliques come together and do something really positive.

I was only peripherally involved. I went to a couple meetings but barely participated. I thought it was awesome and inspiring that all the punks were supporting the woman he'd assaulted. But I didn't feel like I had much of a role to play, because I had drifted out of the scene.

"The Scene" is I suppose a different concept for different people, but I would explain it as this:

You get kicked out of the bar for peeing on the bouncer. Within days, hundreds of people are aware that you got kicked out of the bar for peeing on the bouncer.

The scene is the mechanism for this dissemination of information. It is composed of all the people who go to shows, parties, bars, and subversive meetings. It's the poor urbanite's civil society.

In retrospect, I do not think that I had drifted out of the scene. Actually, I was going out more than ever. I just wasn't hanging out exclusively with punks.

I still played in a band, and I still went to basement punk shows. But work and organizing had come to dominate my social life. When I went out drinking, I usually went with coworkers. Most of them didn't wear studs and none of them wore buttflaps[73], but they were still excellent people and lots of fun. We shotgunned beers, jumped off bridges naked, played backyard ping pong till 5am, and plenty more.

I still had good friends who were punks, and I had good friends who were activists. But they were old friends. All my new friends were coworkers who were helping to create this new union.

Minneapolis is a small city for a metropolis. If you meet somebody at a party, probably you have a mutual acquaintance.

I felt like I was retreating from the scene to do union work, but in reality our JJs union could never exist outside "the scene." The entire city was going to hear about it, and their support or disdain would in turn affect our ability to organize. We weren't operating outside the scene - we were just creating a new sub-community within our larger community. A community based on the principles of solidarity and fighting the bosses.

That's what I believe now, but the whole time I worked at JJs I scoffed at outside opinions. I didn't care what the punks thought about our union, and I had no interest in garnering media attention. All that mattered to me was what my coworkers thought. I believed that if we were successful our actions would speak for themselves, and community support and media attention would follow.

So I continued to disassociate myself with the punks, only occasionally catching up with old friends in the twilight hours around the fire at Medusa or in some filthy basement at a DIY show. The bulk of my free time I spent worrying about how to win a union election at Jimmy John's.

---

[73] Trainhopping armor

Chapter 32
A Summer Frenzy

June 9th, 2010

In other campaign news, Lita quit, some other people quit, job still sucks, etc.

What else? We've been meeting regularly, working on this new petition. I'm supposed to meet with some lawyer.

I've been playing lots of cribbage with Ryan and ping pong with Nick Anton and Micah.

I dunno, nothing too dramatic. Neighbors called the cops on the Shit Biscuit for a show the other day. 5 squads, big hubbub.

Jared's drawing sweet graphics for the campaign, Ayo wrote a letter to the City Pages, Davis is writing the petition, David's working on a timeline, I'm working on the contact list. The committee's pretty strong right now. We just need to do this goddamn petition and go public. That's my opinion.

By June of 2010 we had collected 49 authorization cards signed by workers in our franchise. We had about the same number of cards signed by people who used to work in our franchise. These cards were the result of hundreds of hours of meeting with coworkers and discussing working conditions and the union.

Then it came to our attention that in order to file for an election you need a petition of signatures signed and dated within the last 6 months. Most of our cards were expired. So we tossed them all out and started a new petition.

Which seems like it should have been disheartening but wasn't really. I was pretty used to reinventing the wheel by this point. And really, if somebody from our committee hadn't talked to a person about the union in 6 months it was probably worth doing another 1-on-1 anyway.

Besides, our committee was rocking and rolling[74]. Summer had arrived in Minneapolis and the heat had us darting

---

[74] 1-on-1s, 1-on-1s, 1-on-1s

all over the Twin Cities on our bicycles, dripping sweat and talking union. We had picked up new members, notably:

Micah Barley: Brilliant in both English and German, Micah was into electronic music, mobile dance parties, and god-awful puns[75].

Jaim'ee Bolt: Militant cabaret performer with a big gender-bending heart. Like a queer Liza Minnelli, except shorter blonder and I guess I never heard her sing.

We had set September 1st as our new deadline for going public. This time it really felt like we were going to do it. Labor Day weekend was too convenient to miss. The IWW's annual delegate convention would be in the Twin Cities that weekend, so we'd have a bunch of footloose supporters for any actions we took. And since it was Labor Day it would make an attractive story for media outlets.

Timing aside, I had too much faith in my fellow committee members to believe we'd miss this deadline. Max had transferred to the Block E store and was doing 1-on-1s with all his coworkers there as well as friends of his at the Franklin store. Forman had brought St. Louis Park JJ workers into the committee and was preparing a media strategy. David was meeting with his coworkers at the Skyway store and working on a timeline for going public. Jaim'ee was working at the 9th street store and had brought Ayo back into the campaign. Jared and Robby had all the drivers at Riverside

---

[75]Pun: A play on words:

down with the union. And at Dinkytown Emily, Micah, and myself formed the core of our union's funniest and sexiest shop committee[76].

Davis was our most impressive organizer. When he had started at the Uptown JJs he had reported that everyone in the store was wary of the union because of Brandon's firing after the work stoppage. Within months he had 24 out of 27 workers down with the union. They even held a meeting to design their own schedule, which they submitted to management just like we had done in Dinkytown back in 2007!

That summer I went on tour with Terracide again, but this time when I came back the committee hadn't ceased functioning without me. Quite the opposite! Functioning subcommittees had sprung up, and some committee members were attending multiple meetings a week on top of their sandwich preparation duties.

They'd resurrected War Council and called it War Committee. War Committee meetings were a riot. Meeting places were completely arbitrary. We met at parties, in coffee shops, in some random backyard. We always met super-late — never before 9pm, sometimes as late as midnight. These meetings were laid-back and usually included alcohol. We'd get all riled up and brainstorm direct action tactics, then hang out into the wee hours of the night and let loose with immature drunken shenanigans, as was our right as a bunch of attractive 20-something radicals.

We also struck a Solidarity Committee that became popular amongst students and labor-left types. Since we were about to go public, we wanted to create some infrastructure for outside supporters to contribute. I only went to a couple of those meetings, but I can attest that they were positive, inspiring, and quite a bit more on point and less crude than our War Committee meetings. Davis and Forman were the most active JJ workers on the Solidarity Committee, but then they were active in all of our committees...

---

[76] Well, that's how I remember it...

106

Forman was bottom-lining a media committee, and we also had a quasi-functioning legal committee. I wanted to start calling our larger committee the Jimmy John's Workers Union[77] and create an Organizing Committee that met outside of our regular business meetings and would focus on 1-on-1s.

I had learned my lesson about trying to do too much myself and wanted to focus on helping other committee members develop as organizers. I knew that I could probably collect 20 signatures at the Dinkytown store for our recognition petition, but I decided to let Emily and Micah collect the signatures instead. I figured we'd be stronger as a union if they got the experience doing 1-on-1s, even if it meant slower going in collecting signatures. A hell of an idea, if I may say so myself.

Throughout the summer we organized around our recognition petition and had great success. Problem was, we couldn't agree on what to do with it.

All along I had been adamant about filing for a union election with the Labor Board. But a significant chunk of our committee including a couple of our best organizers were adamant about not participating in the election process.

Forman's idea, for instance, was that we'd go public and demand union recognition. Then we'd carry out a series of escalating direct actions culminating in something dramatic like an occupation until we pressured the company to recognize us. He had visions of barricades and battles.

My more conservative position was that corporate JJs would never stand for the franchise voluntarily recognizing our union and would subsidize it if need be to keep it non-union.

We debated this key decision endlessly and got nowhere. In the end we decided we would go public first and then vote on whether to file for an election. We planned on doing heavy turnout for a mass meeting of JJ workers at the

---

[77] I take no credit for the name, and I doubt anybody would. We defaulted to that after no one came up with anything flashier.

end of August where we would finalize a set of demands. Then the Thursday before Labor Day weekend, delegations of workers in all 9 stores would present our demands to management and we'd go from there.

Chapter 33
Corporatism

August 25th, 2010

Alex signed the petition, said he'd come to the meeting Sunday. Just got off my first shift post Terracide 2010 tour. It went fine. The District which used to be The Melrose is now Stadium View. New computer science building by Washington Ave bridge, new CVS.

The University has changed a lot since I went there. TCF Bank Stadium, no General College, higher tuition, Hanson Hall, the Comp Sci Building, a Science Building on E River Road. Just keeps getting more and more corporate. As do Dinkytown, Stadium Village, and the West Bank. I miss the Dinkytowner.

The Grease Pit closed when I was out of town. Developers.

Jimmy John's was a giant and fast-expanding corporation – at some point while I worked there the 1,000th store opened – but it was organized on a franchise model. There were some corporate-owned stores in Illinois, but the vast majority of JJs were owned by franchisees, in our case Mike Mulligan.

In theory, Jimmy John and all his corporate cronies were not my bosses and had no authority over me. Mike Mulligan signed my checks, and he and his management team decided raises, schedules, firings, etc.

In reality, if Jimmy John came into a store and told a manager to fire me, my manager would fire me.

In 2010 an army of corporate JJs geeks descended on the Dinkytown JJs where I worked. The story was that some senior corporate guy – Jimmy John himself in some versions –

had visited the Dinkytown store and had waited too long to get his sandwich. I suspected the real reason corporate had set up camp was that they'd gotten wind of the union campaign and wanted to investigate and kill it before it was too late.

Whatever the reason may have been, for two months in Dinkytown we had one or more corporate guys working with us every minute of the day. They arrived in 3-person teams and rotated out every two weeks. Two of them would work during the day and one at night.

I only ever met one woman who worked for corporate. The rest were all Caucasian males ages 25 to 40.

They were clean-shaven and wore white polo shirts. They smiled big fake smiles and cheerfully shat out corporate catchphrases. When someone wanted to pay with a credit card they'd chant "Fantastic plastic!" A roast beef sandwich with no tomatoes was a "Deuce no tommy!" They loved talking up their exploits in the hotel bars and always tried to exude an air of hipness.

If there's a hell tailored specifically for me, it's full of corporate JJ bros all dressing talking and walking in the same phony manner.

*

Back when I was in college I remember reading a pamphlet put out by Socialist Alternative called "The Corporate University." It was an academic analysis of the changes taking place at the University of Minnesota, arguing that the university was abandoning its mission of educating young adults in favor of attracting corporate dollars as a research facility.

During my last year at the U I briefly participated in a struggle around the closing of the university's General College. The mission of the General College was to act as an entryway for students from low-income families and failing schools to attend the university. The new president of the university wanted to close it and divert that money towards scholarships for top out-of-state students. This would make the university less accessible and less diverse but more attractive to corporate research bigwigs. I got pepper-sprayed and was on the news, but they closed the General College anyway.

During my years at Jimmy John's I got a street level view of the changes taking place around the university. I delivered sandwiches to construction workers at all the new science buildings they were building. I delivered to numerous new high-priced apartments that looked like condos but were actually just luxury student housing. I also watched small businesses like the Dinkytowner bar close and be replaced by corporate chains. Applebees, CVS, Five Guys, and – Jimmy John's.

The neighborhoods I lived and hung out in seemed to be changing in the same way. Condos went up on 28th and Cedar right in the heart of Phillips. Developers revamped the old Sears building on Chicago and Lake and packed it with businesses, a hotel, and condos. They renamed it the "Midtown Exchange" and suddenly Phillips became Midtown – a much more business-friendly neighborhood.

And of course, new Jimmy John's stores were opening all over town.

In a neighborhood context, people call this trend gentrification. It means developers and government forces colluding to push poor people out of an area and make way for fast-spending yuppies.

In a business context, I'll call the trend corporatism[78]. I have no idea what "corporation" means in American law. But I know what it means to the American working class.

As consumers it means a recognizable brand image that you know will be the same no matter where in the world you find it.

As workers it means working for an imposing faceless entity. In the vast majority of cases workers never even meet

---

[78] Wil suggests to me that this is how Mussolini described Italian fascism. No that is not what I'm implying. Unless it makes sense, in which case sure, pretend I have studied the works of Mussolini.

the big boss – Jimmy John for me. They just know that there is a corporate power structure backed by hundreds of millions of dollars that they'd be foolish to oppose.

*

I've always been fascinated by the Minneapolis skyline. Here you have these massive structures built by countless masses of workers. Left untouched by humans I imagine the skyscrapers would stand for thousands of years, long after the pyramids and Stonehenge have crumbled to dust. In that sense I'm awed by our capabilities.

But also when I look at the skyscrapers I think – these aren't public buildings. They feel like they belong to the city, but they don't. Somebody owns the IDS Center. Somebody owns the Foshay Tower. The Wells Fargo building. Target Headquarters.

While we hustle through the skyways[79] dishing out sandwiches for $7 an hour, we're toiling in some ruling class motherfucker's house. Somebody who resides in that distant almost inconceivable apex of the corporate world where you don't measure square footage in thousands, you measure it in millions.

What would it take for the working class to reclaim what we've built?

To me the answer to that is the same as the answer to gentrification and corporatism. We need a revolutionary mass movement of workers. The real question is – how do you build that movement? I believe in building working class organization through workplace organizing.

The challenge in the 21st century to union organizing is that the scale and structure of business has changed. We live under a form of capitalism dominated by sprawling multinational

---

[79] The skyscrapers in downtown Minneapolis are connected by an elaborate "skyway" system so that lawyers don't have to walk outside during January to travel from their offices to the courtrooms. The skyways are full of corporate chain restaurants, including Jimmy John's.

111

corporations. Walmart is the largest private employer in the world, and no union has the capacity to send organizers into 8,000 Walmarts across 4 continents.

Back before Wil and I had decided to organize at JJs, we had been inspired by the IWW's Starbucks Workers Union (SWU).

The SWU had gone public in New York City in 2004. Their demands were much the same as everyone else's. Better pay, guaranteed hours, respect from management. They marched on their bosses, picketed, circulated petitions, and in one case filed for an election. The union spread to several stores in the New York area, then a bunch of key organizers were fired and the campaign in New York lost steam.

But then something new happened. Wobblies, of their own initiative and without any direction from the SWU, started organizing Sbuxes in cities all across the country and in a few cases overseas. Most of these campaigns never made it too far, but by 2006 there were public union presences in Sbux stores in Chicago and Baltimore. In 2008 the Twin Cities joined the fray.

What SWU organizers had done was combine the loose semi-autonomous structure of a union like the IWW with an organizing campaign built around a brand image[80]. The result was that after the campaign made headlines, aspiring young organizers latched onto the brand and got jobs at Starbucks with the intent of organizing.

To me this is the future of the labor movement. In order to combat these giant sprawling corporations, unions need to be structured in such a way that organizing campaigns can go viral.

When a campaign heats up in one city, radicals in a hundred other cities need to immediately be able to plug in and start their own organizing. Mainstream unions could never organize like this. Their campaigns are created and controlled

---

[80] The idea of organizing around brand images is explored in Naomi Klein's pop-activism smash hit *No Logo*. Convinced me.

by a top-down bureaucracy. You can't just join SEIU and start your own SEIU campaign. You can with the IWW.

Thus I found myself working at Jimmy John's, a place that I would never eat at and honestly considered an eyesore in the neighborhood. I worked with the corporate bro-hood and pretended I adhered to the JJ religion. I asked customers if they wanted to add peppers and encouraged them to buy the #1 (cause that sandwich had the highest profit margin). I was like a reluctant Christian who kneels at church but isn't actually praying.

*

Regardless of why the corporate infestation of the Dinkytown store occurred, the union plowed ahead undeterred. The corporate guys hired a bunch of new workers, which I speculated was an attempt to hinder us from organizing a majority. But a couple of the new workers were already friends of mine, and most of them seemed pretty cool. So really it just gave us a bigger share of the workforce at a store where the union was strong. Fine by me.

After two months the polo-shirted bros packed up shop and skipped town. Work returned to normal. The night shift workers were pouring whiskey in their sodas again. I was cursing up a storm and stapling the oven mitts shut again.

Behind the scenes, in apartments and coffee shops all over town, we were organizing furiously in preparation for our forthcoming mass meeting. As of August 10th we had several petitions scattered across town in various backpacks and folders. Our organizers reported that we had 38 signatures — about 80 short of our goal, with three weeks till our go public date. We had organizers and supporters in all the stores, but outside of Dinkytown where I was focused it was hard for me to gauge the level of union support around the franchise.

Oh well. No turning back now.

Chapter 34
The Mass Meeting

Monday August 30th, 2010

Mass meeting last night at Max's house was huge. 32 JJ workers plus Deeq who'd just quit and Matt from the media committee. 5 wobblies were also there making signs. And a few people from the house were in and out. 40-some people. We had 3 workers from every store except the SLP stores.

The plan is to do marches on the boss in all 9 stores Thursday morning, leaflet outside the stores that day, go to Block E and demand a meeting with Mike, have a huge picket in front of Block E, press conference Friday, small pickets at all 9 stores Friday, bike ride Saturday, actions in SLP Sunday, national pickets Monday.

Lots of work to do this week. And before the week is over this shit's gonna be all over the city and the news and the country.

Many times over the course of the campaign we had decided to do intense turnout for meetings, and it had never gone quite as well as we planned. There's a mathematical guideline in union campaigns that you want to build an organizing committee that's 10% of the overall workforce – about 20 people for us. We had never had 20 JJ workers at a meeting. So I had no reason to expect that our mass meeting would be successful.

We had decided on Max's house for the mass meeting. It was centrally located and Max was universally beloved around town. It had a large open living room that was connected to a large open dining room.

When we finally had our mass meeting, every chair in the house was taken. People were sitting on the arms of couches or on the floor against the walls. Others stood. I'd never seen anything like it. The years of repeated organizing failures had beaten me down to a point where I'd never imagined we could get so many JJ workers in the same room talking about fighting for change. Yet somehow we'd done it.

The meeting was sloppy but about as productive as it could have been given the circumstances. We spent a long time on an initial go-around of grievances. The go-around was necessary, because many people had never been to a union meeting before and were intimidated. Go-arounds force people to speak and participate. Unfortunately they're slow and not all that productive.

Still, an opportunity for me to introduce a few impressive new faces on the committee:

Manuel: Charismatic hip hop artist who had just started at the Franklin store. He had been busted for selling weed and now as a felon was in a bind for employment opportunities. But he didn't give a fuck and jumped right into agitating with his coworkers – a natural organizer.

Jake Foust: Young sarcastic genius of sorts who delivered sandwiches at Riverside. He had been a part of the action that got sexual harasser Mike J. fired from Riverside, and he quickly became one of our most active committee members.

Brittany Kitty: Like Manuel, B.K. got hired right on the eve of us going public and her first impressions of life at Jimmy John's were of a whirlwind of union activity. She was a social justice advocate addicted to all things kitten and a strong voice amongst the inshoppers.

Dan Rude: A punk from Duluth, Rude had transferred to the 9th St. JJs and proceeded to compete for most hungover worker in the franchise. He was similar to Stix in his punctuality problems but down as fuck and militantly pro-union.

Joram Livingood: A friendly roundish churchgoer with a positive outlook that matched his surname, Joram was our most active committee member at Calhoun besides the omnipresent Davis Ritzema.

We had a short agenda of three points. First a set of demands which we could debate and amend. Then a plan of action for the coming week. Finally we were going to break into shops and discuss our plans for going public at our individual stores.

The discussion went poorly. The only way to have democratic discussions with large groups is using strict parliamentary procedure, but we didn't think folks would feel comfortable with that, so it was a bit of a free-for-all. Ultimately we added a couple demands and a couple actions and passed everything unanimously, which told me that people had concerns but didn't voice them[81].

Business aside, the turnout alone made the meeting powerful. I'm sure I was not the only one shocked by the packed house. After attending that meeting, no one could brush the union aside as insignificant or futile. The Jimmy John's Workers Union had arrived.

Chapter 35
Paranoia

September 1st, 2010

Felt terrible this morning. Too hungover to make calls. Wanted to get up at 10 and help Callie Jen and Rachel move. Woke up at 12:30, still drunk, super anxious. Laid down on the couch till I had to go to work, almost. Sent some texts about my concerns over wearing union buttons tomorrow. Glad I did.

Also last night I wrote a super paranoid and stupid email about how we have a rat and the Mulligans know we're going public tomorrow. Fortunately I was too drunk and failed to send it. Just a sec ago I noticed the page "Wiktionary.org – coherent" up in my web browser. That's how I found out that I blacked out. No memory of that and it's humorously fitting. That

---

[81] That's basically how I feel about consensus process, by the way. Either there's an understanding that there's no room for opposition and everything passes unanimously or else somebody blocks everything and nothing gets done.

said, I assume we have a rat and I said as much at two different meetings tonight.

The mass meeting was on Sunday night, and the plan was to go public on Thursday morning. That left a three day window of constant meeting, planning, and panicking.

So many people had attended the mass meeting it was inconceivable that somebody hadn't leaked our plans to the Mulligans. Why hadn't we just gone public on Monday? Were we insane!?

Besides my rat paranoia, I also had major administrative concerns. I said earlier in this account that I wouldn't bullshit a rosy picture of this campaign, so it only seems fair to divulge our administrative shortcomings.

The IWW was well-equipped to organize actions around demands. What the IWW was not well-equipped for was administration. At all levels of the union we constantly had officers resigning, or being charged with negligence, or in some cases – like with the JJWU – we didn't even have officers.

Earlier in 2010 I had pushed hard to establish a set of bylaws for the JJWU that would define a simple decision-making process, membership structure, and officer responsibilities. We had formed a bylaws committee and met a couple times. The bylaws committee could never come to an agreement on the membership issue, so we brought two separate proposals to the larger committee. But in the larger committee we felt we didn't have enough quorum to decide the membership issue either, and eventually we dropped the entire issue of bylaws.

We found ourselves on the verge of going public as a union with no bylaws and very ad hoc everything.

We had elected Davis as our treasurer, but the extent of his authority was unclear. All we knew was that he had to sign the checks.

The membership issue we more-or-less decided but never put in writing. In a contentious and much-criticized decision, we went with a dual membership structure aping that of the Starbucks Workers Union. The way we said it, the IWW had formal membership and the JJWU informal membership. What

117

that meant was that you did not have to join the IWW and pay dues to participate in the JJWU. You could participate in actions and rock a union spoke card and say you were in the union just like everybody else.

That membership structure to me does not seem ideal, but it's a difficult issue.

Standard union practice is to build an organizing committee, win formal recognition, and then when and only when you agree with the bosses on a contract, everybody in the bargaining unit is forced to join the union and the company starts taking union dues out of their paychecks. This is called dues checkoff, and it's banned by the IWW constitution.

So what's the alternate route? We want members in the IWW only if they want to be members. We don't want to force anybody to pay dues. But does that mean that the union will be known as that 10% of the workforce who are active on the committee and willing to pay dues? A majority of workers will never voluntarily pay dues to a union they don't have much time for – this I firmly believe.

Anyway, I don't have a great answer on that one.

But even more distressing to me was our failure to reach a consensus on a recognition strategy. Erik Forman and David Beekie were vehemently opposed to filing for an election with the NLRB. They were also smart and well-spoken.

I was adamant that we should file for a union election. I had spent years meeting with coworkers and asking them to sign authorization cards, and I'd be damned at this late hour if somebody was going to snatch my dream of union recognition away from me. If the committee voted not to file for an election I would respect their decision, but it would be a bitter pill to swallow.

It was an issue that I felt could potentially destroy our committee. We couldn't win an election without Forman and Beekie, and we couldn't pull off any large-scale actions without me. On the eve of going public I met with the two of them and Jaim'ee Bolt to try to reach some sort of compromise and failed miserably. Erik screamed at me and called me a drunk, and I said well you're the one screaming.

So we continued to postpone making a decision on this critical point. But we were running out of time. If we were going to file we had to file immediately after we went public, while we still had momentum.

Besides that meeting, I attended two other meetings in those final three days before going public. First was a solidarity committee meeting, which was uplifting but not too noteworthy.

The second was a Dinkytown shop committee meeting, which was incredibly stressful and difficult to pull together. We met at Rachel, Jen, and Callie's apartment. They were three young fun and attractive inshoppers who worked at Dinkytown. Besides them there were six more of us Dinkytown JJ folks plus Arthur Daniels, who had once signed an authorization card but no longer worked there.

I started the meeting with a sloppy but impassioned monologue about why I believed in the union cause. The meeting proceeded in herky-jerky disorganized fashion including alcohol-induced tangents and Matt Bongers[82] saying he actually thought he made pretty good money there. But we left with a plan of action that seemed to please everyone, and I was relieved that enough workers had been involved in the decision-making that management would not be able to isolate the union organizers in the store.

The following morning Emily, Micah, Callie, and I were going to stop working at 11:15am and deliver our demands to Ryan, our manager. We were going to tell him we'd formed a union, and that he needed to call the owner and let him know we wanted to meet with him.

After the meeting I remember biking home in pouring rain, texting furiously with Erik Forman, telling each other about our shop committee meetings and the other ones we'd heard about. When I reached my porch I called him.

In the black of a stormy thunderous night, Erik and I reminisced on how far we'd come. Three and a half years of 1-on-1s, phone calls, and committee meetings. All the times we'd

---

[82] That name I did not change.

waited at coffee shops for coworkers who never showed up, all the poorly attended committee meetings that left us feeling miserable. All the friends who had burnt out and quit, all the times we'd stopped meeting regularly and given up hope. We had trudged through the muck and shit that is a union organizing campaign, and finally, FINALLY, we could see the green grass on the other side.

Chapter 36
Going Public

For all the explosion of activity that followed us going public as a union, what I remember most vividly is biking over the Washington Avenue bridge on my way to work the morning of Thursday, September 3rd.

It was a cool cloudy morning. I was listening to "Rainbow Connection" by Kermit the Frog on my cellphone, which I always kept strapped to my chest above my U-lock. I had hardly slept but was burning with adrenaline. I dodged students but hardly noticed them. I looked out over the bridge at the mighty Mississippi and thought – this is one of those moments I'll never forget.

Sunday September 5th, 2010

Went public on Thursday. Callie, Micah, Emily, and I turned in our demand letter to Ryan at Dinkytown. He freaked out at first and ran into the office. This after Altan tried to play go-between. I followed him and got Micah and Emily to come with me. I did most of the talking, which was bad. Eventually we just went back to work. He never did call Rob. Rob called him.

At Block E Ricki, Jack, and maybe JJ and/or Bob gave the letter to Kevin. He was chill but told them to give it to Rob themselves. Rob eventually found out and was a wreck. Wouldn't make eye contact apparently.

At Riverside Jake and Jared gave Jay the petition. He gave them the "is this a joke" routine. He doesn't think it's a joke now.

At Calhoun, six workers – Davis, Joram, and I don't know who else surrounded Corey and read our demands, told him what was up. Probably the strongest work stoppage of the day. He called Rob and was later running around the store screaming "fuck" to himself.

Oh, by the end of the day Ryan had read the letter and was totally supportive. We'll see if that lasts.

At 4th St. Jaim'ee, Von, Ben, and Dan surrounded Tim outside his office and delivered their letter. He apparently turned a brilliant shade of green. He called Rob right away. They also put on union pins and have been wearing them ever since. Calhoun is pinned-out too. West End as well.

At West End Erik, Bart, and 3 others (Jane and Candice?) cornered Monica and read almost the entire demand letter, including the fine print (Bart read it). Took several minutes. She was quiet and said she agreed with them.

Then Erik and Bart drove over to Knollwood and along with Jake from that store walked in the back office and delivered the letter to Erik. He tried to stonewall them at first but Forman got up in his face and he listened to them and called Rob.

At Franklin Max, Manuel, and a couple others gave the letter to Missy. They said it went smoothly, she called Rob, and the rest of the day was chill.

At Skyway David, Paulmer, and Dolezal gave the letter to Krysta. I don't actually remember how that went down, but Paulmer was pumped.

At 3 I met up at Dunn Brothers downtown with Ricki, Bob, Jake, David, Davis, Erik, Emily, Max, Jared, Manuel, Jaim'ee, Joram, Gaby, and a couple others. We reported, strategized, and then walked over to Block E. At Block E 15-20 of us all walked past Kevin into the back and up to the franchise office. Kevin was on the phone and made no move to stop us. Davis knocked on the door. "Anybody there? It's the Jimmy John's Workers Union!" Nobody answered so we went outside and started picketing.

The picket got pretty big, probly 100 deep, 200 people over the course of 3 hours. Chris Graham came by – he's not too supportive. Nobody had talked to him. Carson and Alex from Dinkytown walked the line, along with me, Emily, Micah, and Jake. At one point it started pouring rain, and 50 of us (at least) went inside and sat down in the Block E dining area for about 10 minutes.

That night I went to Hard Times, then Palmers, then Chris Graham's housewarming party.

At Hard Times I hung out with Micah then played chess with Ayo. Ricki, Jack, Jake, Jared, Max, and several others were there hanging out. I was in a weird mood and not too social.

At Palmers I hung out with Paulmer, Reuben, Davis, Jaim'ee, and several others. I also ran into Krystyles and Erik. Talked to him about the action at Knollwood and the union briefly. "I'm probably not supposed to be talking to you about this, but I'm interested to see what comes of this." Micah was there too.

Oh, Jeff P. was out in front of Dinkytown leafleting earlier that day. Micah said Jeff made his day. Other supporters / wobblies leafleted the other stores.

Then I went to Chris and Rob Green's house, where Micah was also. Talked a little union, mostly talked life stuff with Rob Green. He lent me a Max Weber book. I'll read it if I have any free time ever again.

Friday Emily and others did a press conference in front of Block E. It got some local coverage. WCCO, KSTP, a few smaller papers. I was at work all day. Got into an argument with Altan about the work stoppage. Really not looking forward to that every day.

Saturday I worked all day, then went and got a beer with Matt Bongers. We waited for the union bike ride to hit Dinkytown and joined it. New guy Drew who I'd spoken with earlier in the day signed the petition. John and Tyrone were pretty excited about it. We were going into stores, chanting "Union" and giving gift bags and balloons.

After that I took the ride on the gravel shortcut at Metalmatic to the Stone Arch Bridge. Then Block E., then Franklin, then Calhoun, where there was a decent-sized picket. I bought a small bottle of whiskey at Franklin instead of going into the store.

I ditched the picket pretty early (and skipped the after party) to go to the last Romp at Bedlam. I went with Brandon of Brandon and Nitali who apparently just joined the military. I got blackout drunk, got jealous of C------'s boyfriend, rode home with M------, fell off my bike, immediately asked her to make out, arrived home with very little dignity. Probly did a bunch of dumb stuff in between.

Today I was super-hungover, ordered lasagna, then ran around getting shit for this rally tomorrow. Then had an epic meeting where we voted to file for an election! It's finally going to happen!

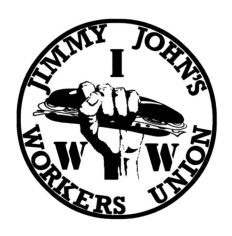

*

The Election

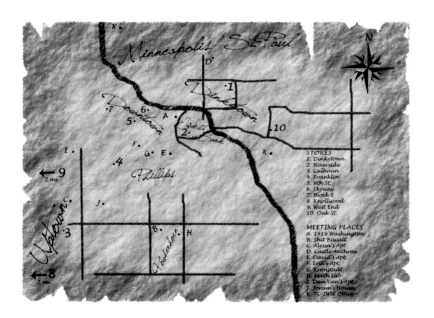

STORES
1. Dinkytown
2. Riverside
3. Calhoun
4. Franklin
5. 9th St.
6. Skyway
7. Block E
8. Knollwood
9. West End
10. Oak St.

MEETING PLACES
A. 1419 Washington
B. Shit Biscuit
C. Alyssa's Apt.
D. Castle Anthrax
E. David's Apt.
F. Erik's Apt.
G. Kronstadt
H. Math Lab
I. Dan Van's Apt.
J. Joram's House
K. TC-IWW Office

September 14th, 2010

Monday we filed the election. Erik Davis showed up at my house at 10:30 while I was cooking eggs, toast, and turkey bacon. A good breakfast. Micah showed up in stripes and suspenders. Max showed up.

Went down to the NLRB office. Erik Davis left to go confront Tim Vaas, 4th St. manager. Budget coffee at "the Pub," waited for Max's RNC8 lawyer[83].

Filing went shittily. I left one of our 14 petitions in the damn copier, and our signature page says nothing about the IWW. I think we'll be okay. I was pretty freaked out at the time though. I realized (which I try not to do, generally) at one point that I was the only one in the office standing, besides the NLRB person. Lawyer wrote up a bunch of affidavits that we haven't done shit with.

Ryan C. called me and I went to Burrito Loco (my current location) and played darts and drank beers. Got too drunk, I guess. Good time with Ryan.

Played some FIFA 2010 in Jimmy's room.

Picked up the Terracide Van, which kinda sucked.

Went to the party at Dan Rude's. My idea actually. Going away party for Jake. I was wasted. I said many things.

Big "Solidarity Forever" moment at that party. I don't know how to think about it. Totally unexpected. I'm generally opposed to old Wobbly songs. That shit was pretty cool though. Ayo, Jake, and Davis called for a "secret announcement" about the rancid food at Calhoun. Or something. We started singing. Nobody knew the verses. Dustin who Max and I signed up at Dan's the other day jumped up on the back of the couch and started singing the verses and swinging his arm. Entire party really into it. Weird.

---

[83] The pro bono lawyer representing Max on his terrorist conspiracy case had agreed to accompany us in filing our election. He knew nothing about labor law but spoke their language and had a closet full of suits.

Chapter 37
Pickets and Parties

The first couple weeks after we went public felt festive at work. Union supporters were wearing JJWU buttons on their work shirts, delivery guys had JJWU spoke cards on their bicycles, and management didn't know what the hell to do. We had made our demands, the owners had refused to negotiate with us, and we had proceeded to publicly stuff our union down their throats.

Union members held a rally on campus with hip hop artists and DJs, then marched over to the Dinkytown store and picketed outside while I was working.

It was the end of the day shift and most of my coworkers had already been cut. I was kicking it behind the cold table with my manager and three coworkers, none of whom were strong union supporters, watching this raucous picket out in front of the store and trying to decide what it all meant.

I stuck to our issues and argued for the picket on the lines that it was a pressure tactic meant to force the Mulligans to concede. "If they're not going to negotiate a

regular raise schedule with us, then we'll keep showing up in front of their stores en masse and airing all their dirty laundry to the public."

At the end of the day though, I wasn't much in favor of these outsider pickets myself. Altan, the voice of anti-union sentiment in my store, criticized the pickets for being composed of people who didn't work at Jimmy John's. On the one hand, I thought it was great that community members supported us and were willing to come out and march around hooting and hollering.

On the other hand, I agreed with Altan. The purpose of organizing is to build workers power. How does it build workers power to have a bunch of people picketing out in front of a store while all the workers are inside working? Even if it frightens the owners, it doesn't strengthen the union inside the stores and really can only alienate workers who aren't participating in it. That's my opinion anyway. I would increasingly argue against public pickets of outside supporters, and as time went on we did less and less of them.

A more practical picket we organized happened at the Oak Street construction site about a mile from my store in Dinkytown. The Mulligans were about to open their 10th store there, next to the new TCF Bank college football stadium. We thought that if we could effectively hinder their construction schedule we could use it as a chip in bargaining. So a bunch of us got up at 5am and biked onto campus to march around and try to block trucks for a few hours.

That picket was fireworks and a lot of fun. We talked to construction workers and tried to convince them to honor our picket line and stop working. That pissed off their bosses, who puffed out their chests at us and tried to scare us away. Wobblies don't scare easily though, so they called the university cops. The cops came and tried the same routine. Watching Erik Forman go toe to toe with big burly officers and educate them on workers rights is a blast.

The cops got red in the face telling us we couldn't talk to truck drivers and tell them to stop working. Forman stayed calm and told them yes we can and we're going to, so get the hell out of our way. He was a bit more articulate. The cops conceded but did convince us that they'd arrest people if we blocked trucks from entering the site, which defeated the purpose of the picket. So a few folks biked down to the building trades union office[84] and asked them to endorse our picket. The union bureaucrats didn't bite, and ultimately the store was built despite our efforts. Still, picketing for a purpose is much more invigorating than picketing just to be seen.

During the day when I wasn't picketing I was usually working. The dull monotony of spreading mayonnaise and wrapping sandwiches had given way to an exciting new work environment where all day we were cracking jokes about the owners and the union, talking politics and speculating on what the JJWU could accomplish.

Altan and my general manager Ryan, who were my pipelines to management discussions, assured me that the Mulligans believed we lacked sufficient support to file for a union election. I thought that was hilarious. We easily had enough support to file an election. The real barrier to filing came from within our core committee.

The Sunday after we had gone public we finally had the meeting where we voted on filing for an election. It was a grueling 3-hour meeting on comfy chairs and couches in my living room. 15 people showed up, which wasn't as many as I'd hoped but definitely felt like quorum.

For me it was the tensest meeting I'd ever attended. The election was everything to me, and if we voted not to file I'd have

---

[84] Construction work = "the building trades," a small but significant % of which is unionized and has easily locatable (in this age of smart phones and smarter wobblies) union offices.

to live with it.

Forman gave a long insightful monologue about all the reasons we shouldn't file. If we did, we'd be playing by their rules. We'd be taking the struggle out of the workplace, where we're strongest, and placing our fate in the hands of lawyers and government-appointed judges. The Mulligans might be able to draw out the process with hearings and appeals, and we might be stuck in limbo for years waiting for an election. Finally, of course, we might lose. To lose an election would be beyond demoralizing. All the momentum we had built would dissipate. It would affirm the owners in their stance that they couldn't negotiate with us and that we didn't represent the workers.

I followed Forman's speech with a less polished but more passionate appeal of my own. Without recognition, we had no legitimacy. The Mulligans would still give in to some of our demands – raises, job security, fair scheduling – but they would never give the union credit, and neither would the public. To the rest of the world, without recognition we were a failed union campaign.

And so what if we had to play their game by their rules. We were a different kind of union, organized completely from within and with solid shopfloor leaders. We had on our committee some of the strongest smartest people I'd ever met. The company could try all the backhanded sleazy anti-union tactics they could imagine and we'd win anyway. Fuck em.

We took a break before the vote and I went outside and smoked. Max reassured me that they'd "get me my election, but then I had to be down to do badass direct actions." Max was of the opinion that we could file for an election but still focus on organizing actions to win our demands, and his was the popular opinion that carried the vote. When we finally voted I couldn't watch – I closed my eyes. The tally was close – 8 for, 5 against, with 2 abstentions. It was on.

When the sun had set and I had finished working and/or picketing for the day, it seemed like every night there was a union party.

129

The 1419 space[85] where committee member Ben Yella lived put on a union benefit show. Jeff from Block E JJs and Manuel from Franklin JJs performed with their hip hop group True Mutiny. I drank beers on the roof and had long inspiring talks with my coworkers. Everywhere I saw sexy 20-something-year-olds wearing JJWU t-shirts with the sandwich enclosed in a fist. A thrilling combination of hormones and revolutionary fervor.

Wil and I went to a Socialist Alternative party that they had thrown to raise money for us. I'm embarrassed to say we were huge dicks. We took over DJing, talked shit about socialism, and stole their beer. This after they had tried to raise money for us. Whoops...

I dressed as the 2 of Clubs for a Disney-themed party that was full of Dinkytown JJs workers[86] and had a long conversation about work with my coworker Mulan[87]. Tinkerbell and the Aristocats were all about the union, Tarzan and Mowgli were skeptical.

When union member Jake Foust left for Washington we had a big going away party for him at union member Dan Rude's house. Everyone was joining the IWW, everyone was singing union songs, and we all vowed we'd have each other's backs at work or otherwise. It was a good time to be a wobbly.

Chapter 38
The Union Busters

September 21st, 2010

Just got done playing cribbage with Micah post-Captive Audience Meeting. Big turnout for the meeting at Dinkytown – 15 or so workers. Watched a 20-minute film about collective bargaining. No coffee and donuts.

They've started doing captives. Block E and Franklin yesterday. Manuel and Max apparently put our lady union

---

[85] Communal living / art / showspace in 7 corners
[86] It's my favorite card and I swear it's in Alice in Wonderland.
[87] Jen Arbelius

buster on the spot. I did somewhat. "What could we possibly lose in negotiations? We don't have holidays." Something like that. Also, "The IWW doesn't have professional negotiators. Our negotiator will be someone in this room."

While we were picketing and partying, our boss Mike Mulligan was talking to lawyers and shopping for union busters. The firm he settled on was called Labor Relations Institute. They flew out two of their star scumbags - Rebecca Smith and Joe Brock - to break our spirit and defeat our union in the election.

They were two middle-aged suits who claimed to have been organizers for the Teamsters who had seen the light and quit their unions. This was not entirely true.

A couple Twin Cities wobs did some digging on these characters and called their old locals. Rebecca Smith had apparently been paid by the Teamsters to do trainings on asbestos safety and forklift operating. Joe Brock had been a union bureaucrat who was paid to be a union bureaucrat. Both of them had been kicked out of their unions and subsequently found work as union busters.

WHO ARE THESE PEOPLE?

Rebecca Smith and Joe Brock claim that they just want to give us information so we can decide for ourselves if we want to form a union. The truth is that they are from **Labor Relations Institute, Inc.**, a third-party anti-union company hired by Mike and Rob Mulligan. LRI promises employers that if they are hired, workers will be unable to form a union, **or your money back**. Their standard fee is $3000 per day, $375 an hour. Do you think the Mulligans pay these people hundreds of dollar an hour to be a neutral source? Since September 15, we estimate they have been paid $45,000 by the Mulligans, or enough to give every Jimmy Johns worker $200 cash. In a recent campaign against workers organizing a union at Soaring Eagle Casino, LRI made $1.5 million total for their work. Rebecca Smith and Joe Brock have a financial interest in convincing you to vote no. They have a history of using misrepresentations, lies, and subtle threats to divide and conquer workers. Do they deserve our trust? No!

Here is more information about this pair that they have been hiding.

Rebecca Smith	Joe Brock
• Claims to have worked as a union organizer. We contacted the Teamster union local she worked for when she lived near Pahrump, NV. They said she never worked as a union organizer. She ran a program that taught people things like asbestos safety and forklift driving. That means she's lying to us.	• Claims he was a union organizer. The truth is he was a highly paid official, not an organizer.
• Claims she voluntarily quit her paid position in the Teamsters union. The truth is her own coworkers petitioned to have her removed from union office because of her gross incompetence	• Was happy to earn more than $80,000 per year from the Teamsters, then took a pay raise to attack the union members who gave him such a comfortable life style.
• Was paid $103,031 for her work in a union-busting campaign at the Soaring Eagle casinos in Michigan in 2007. What did you get paid in 2007? Rebecca Smith gets a fat salary for union-busting, but she doesn't know and doesn't care about what our lives are like.	• Claims to be a Teamster who left because of problems in the labor movement. He doesn't tell us that he lost an election for office and then sued over losing. The Department of Labor ruled Brock's claims against his local were baseless. So he quit and became a professional union buster.
• Kicked out of her own union, Rebecca Smith now travels around the country making misleading and manipulative statements about unions for employers	• Claims his job as an anti-union consultant lets him help workers improve their lives on the job. Do you really think the Mulligans all of a sudden decided bring Brock for $3,000 per day to improve conditions? Brock is not here to improve workers' lives. He is here to earn a buck preventing us from having more input into how this place is run.

These are the facts. Decide for yourself, who do you trust? Highly paid outsiders like Rebecca Smith and Joe Brock, or your own co-workers who want all Jimmy John's employees to have more voice on the job?

That's par for the course in the "labor relations consulting" industry.

There's a tried and true playbook for union busting, and Rebecca and Joe didn't bother to add any creative wrinkles.

The first step - working over the owner - I can only speculate on since I wasn't there. Before they bill the company hundreds of thousands of dollars they have to justify their service. I mean, wouldn't it be cheaper and easier to just give us raises?

I presume they presented Mike Mulligan with horror stories of companies going out of business after unions came in, upper crusties declaring bankruptcy and applying for jobs at department stores, etc. Then they bragged about their election track record and showed how their work had led to record profits. The Mulligans, in their vulnerable state, ate up the story and opened their checkbooks.

Step two is organizing the managers to fight the union. I wasn't present for this either but heard anecdotal evidence. They immediately instituted a schedule of mandatory manager meetings during which they pounded into our managers' heads that the union was a devious plot to undermine their authority and cause discord at work.

My general manager Ryan told me a story about how at one of these early meetings they had passed around a confidentiality agreement and told all the GMs to sign it. After everyone signed it they pointed out the fine print at the bottom that said "I am a communist and organizer with the Industrial Workers of the World" – illustrating how easy it was for union organizers to trick workers into signing petitions that they actually opposed.

To this point everything went according to script. Except for a few of our friends, most managers became terrified of the IWW.

It wasn't until Rebecca and Joe brought their anti-union bullshit into the shops and had to face union members that I think they realized they might be in trouble.

Soon after we went public we started receiving letters with our paychecks. They were signed by Mike and Rob Mulligan, but I'm certain the union busters wrote them. The first letters we got were pretty standard anti-union lit, the main point being that the union is a 3rd party. A quote:

"The IWW wants to insert itself between our store employees and our leadership team. The presence of an outside third party would destroy the direct relationship we have with each other. It would be contrary to one of the core values that make Jimmy John's successful: One-on-one relationships that value employees and individuals..."

Once we filed for an election, the union busters started holding captive audience meetings. Another anti-union standard, captives are mandatory work meetings where the union busters explain to you why you don't want a union.

The first captive I attended was at 9am on a Saturday morning in Dinkytown. Micah and I were eating Sun Chips out of those insanely loud biodegradable Sun Chips bags. They made us watch a 20-minute video on collective bargaining. It was absolutely ridiculous.

The video looked like it was from the 80s – mullets and bushy hair. A suit at a desk explained some common elements of collective bargaining agreements, then cut to testimonials from workers who said that the union had bargained away pre-existing perks. For example, a guy said that after the union came in he lost his paid holidays and had to start paying dues.

First of all, we didn't have any benefits to lose. We were working for minimum wage with no healthcare, no paid time off, and no time and a half under any circumstances. We didn't even get free sandwiches. Conditions could not possibly get any worse.

But also the workers in this video and the union staffers they showed didn't connect with the JJWU at all. We were young 21st century service industry workers, not middle-aged moustached Teamsters. Most of the workers at my store laughed at the video and wrote off the union busters as shitheads.

At other stores organizers had heated confrontations with the union busters and they cut the meetings short. Rebecca and Joe were used to combating union drives led by paid staff organizers who didn't work in the shops. They weren't used to arguing with union organizers in cramped restaurant dining areas.

Two minutes into one captive at the 9th Street store my friend Reuben asked union buster Joe Brock if he'd ever heard of the rock band Garbage. Joe said, uh, yeah. Reuben said - cause that's what this is! Fucking garbage! Meeting over. Probably the shortest captive he'd ever done.

And then there were a couple stores where hardly anybody showed up to the meetings anyway. Manuel said only 5 people showed up at Franklin. At Oak St. some of the new hires told me they didn't even know the meetings were happening. The meetings were supposed to be mandatory, but as is the case with any work policy, if enough people ignore the policy there's no way to enforce it.

Those first few weeks I was confident that the union busters were totally unprepared for us.

Chapter 39
Tip Jars and Rancid Food

September 28th, 2010

Thursday and Friday we'd done a phone zap on Jason Effertz about the meat incident. Not sure how many people participated, but it was apparently enough, because Sunday morning Rob called Margaret and said her job was not in jeopardy. Also earlier in the week a bunch of people had called the city, who came in and made JJs throw out all the meat sliced that day.

Sunday met up at Suburban World with Davis, Aaron K., Erik Davis, David, and a few other supporters. Drank a bloody mary and watched some of the Vikings game, then walked across the street to Calhoun JJs and presented Margaret with flowers and a giant thank you card we had all signed at a party the night before.

Margaret was super-gracious and embarrassed, did an interview out front while I ran a couple deliveries for her[88].

---

[88] I did the deliveries off the clock in a JJWU t-shirt. Turns out working for free when it's against the rules is more fun than working for pay.

134

The GM Corey flipped out so we had Erik Davis go in and chat with him.

As September rolled on and the union busters bombarded us more and more with anti-union literature and rhetoric, the JJWU did very little in response. We were determined to conduct an offensive campaign and not get caught up in trying to disprove the bullshit the busters were spewing. I believe this was absolutely the right approach.

For instance, the union busters were talking about dues check-off and unions rights clauses. They were trying to convince everyone that if we won the election the IWW would start taking dues out of their paychecks. This was incredibly misleading for multiples reasons:

1. The company would have to agree to a unions rights clause and dues check-off
2. The workers would have to vote to accept a unions rights clause and dues check-off
3. Dues check-off is banned by the IWW constitution

But instead of arguing the points that the union busters wanted to argue, we argued the issues that we cared about. The issue wasn't union dues, it was tip jars.

For some reason or other corporate JJs had a policy against tip jars. That policy pissed off absolutely every worker at JJs. So we made leaflets and organized a franchise-wide action about tip jars.

Once a year every JJs franchise has a dollar sub day. Corporate guys come in to help out, everybody works, it's insanely busy all day, and nobody gets any breaks. Basically you work twice as hard for the same pay and have to spend all day with the corporate brohood. It sucks.

I'd seen a similar promotion at Ben and Jerry's, but when they had dollar cone day they set out tip jars and at least made a shitload of tips. Why not at Jimmy John's?

We bought a thousand plastic cups and spent a night drinking beers and writing "TIPS" in permanent marker on all of them. Then on dollar sub day we had two people outside each of the 10 stores in the franchise passing the cups out along with leaflets explaining our tip cup grievance. We asked the customers to set the tip cups on the counter when they bought their sandwiches.

I was working in Dinkytown along with a couple corporate douches and Rob Mulligan, the owner's son and district manager. As soon as we opened, tip cups started appearing on the counter. Slowly but surely they kept multiplying, until the counter was covered in them. Rob flipped out and tried taking them down, but they kept on coming and eventually he surrendered and let them stay.

The tip jar action was the most popular action the union had done, and the company had no response to it.

Another cool action we did was in defense of our coworker Margaret. Margaret was a 23-year-old sweetheart with fantasy tattoos and dilated pupils. I had lived with her for several months until she and her boyfriend got their own place. I can attest that she was friendly to everyone and always did her dishes.

Margaret had been promoted to PIC[89] and had to open the Calhoun store twice a week. One day she came in and

---

[89] PIC stood for "person in charge." It was a shift supervisor position, the lowest rung of the managerial ladder. After intense debate we had voted to include them in the bargaining unit. The company would have wanted

noticed that the three-door refrigerator where we stored unsliced meat had broken during the night. The meat was all warm and smelled bad. She called her district manager Jason Effertz, who told her he was sending somebody down with bags of ice and that she should slice the meat anyway. Margaret refused to slice the meat and called the city. So her GM Corey drove to the store, sliced the meat himself, and Margaret went home. Then the city inspector came by and made them throw all the meat out anyway.

Margaret was worried she was going to be fired, which seemed incredibly unfair, so we flew into action. We organized a phone zap where a bunch of people called DM Jason's cell phone and told him he shouldn't discipline Margaret for trying to protect customers. Then we marched into her store while she was working and presented her with flowers and a giant thank you card.

The action worked — Margaret kept her job and was allowed to transfer to the Skyway store when she complained about harassment from her GM. She was also very appreciative of the union, as were her coworkers at the Uptown store.

In the IWW we have a cliché: "Direct action gets the goods." Another popular cliché: "The best defense is a good offense." Both apply here.

We weren't going to win a union election by writing essays on collective bargaining. Even if we did win the election, we weren't going to win any concessions by reasoning with our bosses across a negotiating table.

Direct action — workers taking action to directly confront their bosses — is how we win our demands, and it's how we build our union. It's also an approach that the American labor movement seems to have completely abandoned.

---

to include them anyway, which could have led to a hearing and delay. We also thought that after the election we'd be stronger with the PICs on our side.

THE OFFICIAL NEWSLETTER OF THE JIMMY JOHN'S WORKERS UNION

ISSUE No 1
OCTOBER 3, 2010

JJWU HELPS SAVE WORKER'S JOB; ROTTEN BUSINESS PRACTICES EXPOSED!

When Margaret Brickley, Jimmy John's worker and shift supervisor, arrived at work early Monday morning on September the 13th at the Uptown Jimmy John's, she noticed something out of the ordinary. As she began her opening duties she noticed that all of the meat, cheese, and produce that was kept in the main cooler was warm. She checked the cooler; it was broken. Realizing the risk she would be taking by selling the meat to customers, her first reaction was to throw everything away. But being a shift supervisor, Margaret didn't have the authority to make that call. So instead she contacted two of her higher-ups, general manager Cory Reeves and district manager Jason Effortz. After "testing" the meat with a thermometer, Effortz determined that it was suitable for consumption and gave the go ahead to have it sliced and ready to sell. Margaret, disgusted with the final verdict, left early that day refusing to be a part of this unsanitary occurrence.

What eventually took place over the next couple of days was shocking. The following morning, the Minneapolis Department of Health and Safety sent an inspector over to the Uptown Jimmy John's after receiving complaints about the situation. Roughly **80%** of the meat that Margaret had refused to sell was, according to the health inspector, spoiled. Thanks to Margaret and the In-

Chapter 40
Working Poor

September 29th, 2010

Good news and bad news.

The bad news – I have a torn meniscus in my knee and I can't ride my bike. And I don't have enough money to pay my bills. Fuck.

The good news is Wil Olson just finished laying out the first We Are The Union poster for us! I can't wait to see it and I am really excited that I found a way for Wil to get involved again.

Last night I hung out at the Shit Biscuit with Ayo and Wil and Stix and it was pretty inspiring. Stix took a picture for the poster and solved the layout problem (cluster the photos, have the quotes free-floating). He also said he was going to work on Justin at Skyway, think he's the PIC. Fuck yeah! We ended the night by watching all 8 rounds of the Rumble in the Jungle super-wasted with Japanese commentary. That fight's so amazing.

Today I was really tired, but all was good until coming back from a delivery my knee start hurting to where I could no longer pedal. Fuck. I can't afford to take time off right now, either for myself financially or for the union. I'll try driving my car, but it's about to die too. Fuck! I guess I'll just have to battle it until the election, then maybe I can take some time off for it to heal.

Towards the end of September I ran into a couple obstacles in my life and organizing.

First my knee started hurting bad enough to where I could no longer bike. Knee injuries are pretty common with bike delivery — almost all my fellow bike delivery guys had knee trouble at one time or another. I didn't have enough money in my bank account to pay rent and bills, so I just kept working.

Second my computer died and I didn't have any money to fix it. The processer was fried, at which point you can't do much with a desktop besides stack junk on it. But I needed access to e-mail and photoshop and spreadsheets. So I went to Hard Times and used Ayo's laptop. Or I went to a meeting and used David's. Or I drove to B.K.'s house and used hers.

When you're broke as fuck you get used to making do.

The entire time I'd worked at JJs I'd never been able to save any money. For the first couple years I'd put my student loans on deferment, but you can only do that so long before the banks want their money. Since then every year I'd had close to $1,000 in my account at the beginning of the year when I got my tax return. Then I'd watch it disappear until by Halloween I was eating Ramen noodles and spending my last dollar on a cup of Hard Times coffee.

When you're poor you always want to think about how things could be worse. At least I live in a house with heat and running water. At least I'm not starving. At least I have a job. At least somebody somewhere is worse off than me. Nobody wants to consider themselves poor. That's why 99% of Americans call themselves middle class.

At some point though, when you're living below the poverty line, it's hard to deny that times are tough. And everybody at Jimmy John's was living below the poverty line. We all qualified for food stamps. I'd seen enough sob stories at

139

Jimmy John's to last a lifetime. People working for pennies under insane circumstances. A sample from my journal in 2009:

So today I worked with Erik, Mia, Thor, and Jonita. Mia is 17 years old, working full time for $6.75/hr, and 8 months pregnant. Thor was limping around on what he thought was a sprained knee (he slipped on a wet floor the previous night at work), and Erik had been working since 6am and had to go downtown after work to give a DNA sample to the government. Apparently all felons need their DNA on record now. Ricky, the assistant manager, just got out of the hospital (she was having seizures) and is under doctor's orders not to work, but came in for an 8 ½ hour shift anyway. And in the next 3 days she will work 34 hours. Me, I went to bed on an empty stomach last night and didn't get to eat until 4pm today, because we were understaffed and I had to bust my ass all day.

Jimmy John's wasn't special. Maybe we had more chaotic scheduling than some restaurants, but I'd seen the same poverty at every pizza place I'd ever worked too. At Ginelli's Pizza I saw a small business owner tear up a dollar bill and throw it on the floor, and I saw my coworker crying while he made her sweep it up. I saw a homeless coworker taking advances on his check to where he wasn't even getting paid anymore, he was just working to pay off debt.

Poverty is the norm in food service, and it's ugly. That's why we were organizing. Our entire lives we'd watched the American economy become more and more concentrated in the service sector, and we'd seen the service sector become dominated by giant corporate chains. Everywhere the brands went, poverty came with them. There was no point in trying to organize these chains – especially in fast food – because it was impossible. But the IWW believed that no industry was unorganizeable, and we were out to prove it.

Months earlier Forman had started floating an idea about making "We Are The Union" posters. Apparently it was a

140

common union practice in election campaigns. The concept was you'd take pictures of union supporters and collect quotes from them about why they wanted a union. The union busters could say what they want - we were going to talk about all the dirty secrets of working poor in America.

For some reason I was late getting on board with the posters, but after we filed for the election I finally decided what a brilliant idea they were and pushed to make the posters the focal point of our election strategy. Pictures and quotes meant doing 1-on-1s, which as always was what we needed to do anyway.

We began calling our Sunday meetings the JJWU business meetings and struck a separate Organizing Committee responsible for making sure we did 1-on-1s with every worker in the franchise. I volunteered to bottomline the collection of pictures and quotes for the posters.

Wil Olson agreed to do the layout for the posters, which affected me deeply. Wil and I had started the union effort, and when he had lost hope it had broken my heart. Hardly anybody on the committee in Fall 2010 even knew who he was, and maybe it would have been more strategic to task the layout of posters to some new committee member.

But for me it was important to have Wil involved in some way at this critical time. I had seen so many friends burn out and lose faith in the union. To see a spark of hope rekindled in my best friend's eyes brought me strength, strength that I would need as the election neared and the anti-union campaign intensified.

WE ARE THE UNION

"Because this will bring respect and a higher standard of living to the service industry."
Davis Ritsema

"To make history!"
David Boehnke

"Because I need money for school."
Callie Bensel

"Because I'm tired of seeing my coworkers mistreated for being sick."
Jaim'ee Bolte

"Cause I've never seen my bosses sweat at work."
Tim Roach

"The Union is our Song!"
Dan Rude

"Because I have $20 to live on for 2 weeks every paycheck."
Gaby Gagnon

"For all the parents working hard for minimum wage to feed their kids."
Paulmer Johnson

"Because I can't afford my bills."
J.J. Mangen

"Our spirits need a lift and our workers need a raise."
Ayo Collins

"Help the Union! Help yourself!"
Jesse Soderstrom

"I will never feel pressured to deliver sandwiches during a tornado warning again."
Emily Przybylski

"Because people can't afford to take time off or go to the doctor when they're sick."
Erik Forman

"Because we shouldn't have to be scared of the bosses."
Max Specktor

"Because 3.5 million fast food workers could use a little inspiration."
Mike Wilklow

"Friends - let's end this corporate tyranny together!"
Nico Waryran

"We depend on these jobs for our livelihood and deserve a livable wage."
B.K. Koppy

"Two years at minimum wage...That sucks."
Micah Buckley-Farley

"For all my coworkers who I've grown to love."
Von G. Berry

VOTE FOR YOUR COWORKERS.
VOTE FOR YOURSELF.
VOTE UNION OCTOBER 22nd!

Chapter 41
Red Baiting

October 3rd, 2010

Well, Wednesday I got shit-faced. First at B Loco with Micah, Ryan, Callie, Tyrone, and Tony Jeff. Ryan was taking pictures of people and I confronted him about it. He said it was just so our faces would come up in his phone when people called him. I'm not sure I believe him. Names to faces for the union-busters, I think. Fuck it.

Went over to Noah's that night and got blackout drunk. I talked to Manuel and Jeff a bit — they were trying to get me to freestyle rap. I stayed out way too late playing pool. Came home and had some blacked-out argument / discussion with Stix that I can't remember. He was freaked by the Captives.

Thursday started out pretty rough. Super-tired, super-hungover, and I swear Tyrone flinched when I said hi to him. He had just been at Dinkytown's red-baiting Captive, which I was not invited to. I got more comfortable as the day went on though. D$ stood up for the Sabocat, which was cool. Argued with Altan way too much. At the end of the shift, me Ryan, Altan, and D$ were talking about Dinkytown JJs with pride and solidarity, and that was kinda cool.

On the last day of September I came into work and immediately felt the tension. The union busters had started splitting up workers into groups they viewed as strong union supporters and not so strong. That morning they'd given a presentation at our store about how the IWW was a scary violent anarchist / communist / whatever-else organization that wanted to overthrow capitalism.

I didn't know anything about it until my coworker Detrick told me. He didn't think the union busters should have hated on the black cat. He thought the black cat was cool. I asked and turned out the captive had a bunch of slides on the IWW's mascot – the Sabocat – which is a black cat symbolizing sabotage.

The union busters also read the preamble to the IWW's constitution, which begins like this:

"The working class and the employing class have nothing in common. There can be no peace so long as hunger and want are found among millions of the working people and the few, who make up the employing class, have all the good things of life.
Between these two classes a struggle must go on until the workers of the world organize as a class, take possession of the means of production, abolish the wage system, and live in harmony with the Earth."

The IWW is a radical union dedicated to the abolition of the wage system, and any IWW campaign that makes a big enough stink will eventually have to deal with red-baiting. Luckily in the 21st century red-baiting is not all that effective.

I always told people that the IWW welcomed all "isms." Max was an anarchist. Davis

was a socialist. Forman was a syndicalist. I didn't identify as any of these "ists," but I was an adamant anti-capitalist and felt very strongly about democratic procedure. Other members of our committee had mixed feelings about capitalism but still wanted raises.

And at the end of the day, whoop-de-fucking-doo. Red-baiting isn't about having an intelligent debate on how to organize society. It's about trying to strike fear into workers by painting union organizers as crazy dangerous reds who can't be trusted.

The best way to beat off those attacks is to not act crazy. If you're an anarchist, tell your coworkers you're an anarchist. If they want to know why, tell them why. As long as you treat people with respect and offer them solidarity, it's rare that anyone will dislike you for your politics.

My own ideas on "isms," in brief:

I believe that communism was the great tragedy of the 20th century. You can call it Stalinism, Maoism, whatever. All across the world in the 20th century, revolutions occurred that promised worker-run societies but became oppressive dictatorships. Idealists were murdered, and corrupt politicians prospered. On both sides of the iron curtain you had ruling class motherfuckers hijacking egalitarian words like "communism" and "democracy" and rendering them meaningless.

My one sentence explanation for why communism failed in the 20th century: The communist organizations that led the revolutions had undemocratic structures.

There was this international communist movement made up of millions of idealistic revolutionaries who wanted to deliver the world to the workers. But the Communist parties were undemocratic – meaning individuals became engrained in leadership positions. It's really that simple.

So when communists did find themselves in control of countries they ended up just replacing one ruling class with another. Most leftists became Stalin/Mao/Castro apologists and convinced themselves that these communist dictatorships weren't oppressive. Western capitalists pointed out that they were oppressive, and the workers of the world continued to get fucked over by all ruling parties.

But the cold war is over.

I belong to the first post-cold war generation. I remember running around my trailer park in 3rd grade calling kids "commies." I also remember my 4th grade teacher telling us that the giant country called the U.S.S.R. in our atlases didn't actually exist anymore.

Maybe to the average American "communism" is still a scary word, but I don't think it carries the same weight that it

145

once did. I think in the 21st century we have more space in the United States to discuss the ideals of all the various revolutionary "isms," and I think that's a debate that union organizers should welcome.

In any case, the Jimmy John's Workers Union didn't spend much time worrying about red-baiting. You want to call us anarchists? Fine. Wanna calls us commies? Whatever. We made copies of the IWW constitution available in the stores to people who wanted to read about our union's democratic structure. We spoke with pride about the history of the IWW — like Bill Haywood refusing to speak at a union hall during the Bread and Roses strike unless the hall was desegregated. Mostly we kept talking about wages and working conditions. Unfortunately, the union busters finally got the point and started hitting on those issues too.

Around the time they started red-baiting us, we received a letter with our paychecks that told us that if we voted for the union nobody would get raises until we negotiated a contract. They quoted labor law and then intentionally lied about what it meant:

"If employees have voted to have a union as their collective bargaining representative, numerous decisions of the NLRB and the courts make it unlawful for an employer to change the 'status quo.' In other words, the employer may not lawfully change the wages of individual employees under a discretionary merit policy like ours."

This was far more effective union busting than any red-baiting. It was also illegal and misguiding and it made me goddamn furious. I got red in the face explaining to my coworkers that the company couldn't institute a wage freeze, that to do so was the fucking definition of deviating from the 'status quo.'

We filed an unfair labor practices (ULP) charge about that letter, but the rub with ULPs and really the entire labor law system in the United States is that the company has very

146

little to lose and the workers have very little to gain. Even if we won the charge, best case scenario was that the Labor Board would invalidate the election results and we could go through the process all over again, still without union recognition. Then the company could break the law again, we could file a charge again, etc.

The NLRB election process means playing by their rules. If the union breaks the law, the election is invalid and you don't win recognition. If the company breaks the law, the election is invalid and you don't win recognition.

The company always breaks the law, so the only way to win recognition is to accept their illegal actions and win the vote anyway. That was the game.

As September turned to October, for the first time I realized that we could lose this election.

Chapter 42
Media

IWW TAKES ON JIMMY JOHN'S

◀ UNION FROM D1

He's got a point there, organized labor experts say.
Fast food tends to attract young workers who may also be going to school and who

"You are constantly re-educating new workers" about the union, Budd said.
So most conventional unions view fast-food workplaces like Jimmy John's as a losing investment.

《 MAYBE IT TAKES SOMETHING ... LIKE THE IWW, TO HAVE THE COURAGE OR CRAZINESS 》 TO UNIONIZE FAST-FOOD WORKERS.

John Budd, labor relations expert

October 16th, 2010
Before that was New York Times photo opportunity at Dinkytown JJs. That was great. Erik set it up, right at shift change. Emily and Micah were interviewed back on Wednesday about the union and the New York Times flew a photographer down 3 days later to take their picture.

But since it was at shift change there were a lot of workers there and I flew into action...

I never had much interest in dealing with the media. During 1-on-1s I used to tell my coworkers that when we won recognition we'd get our own Wikipedia page. Besides that I didn't much care. I figured if we were able to accomplish the monumental task of winning union recognition at an American fast food franchise, the media recognition would take care of itself.

While media is certainly not the most important element of a union campaign, it does in retrospect seem essential to what we were trying to accomplish. We wanted the JJWU to inspire workers in other cities, and in order for that to happen they had to hear about it. Luckily we had Erik Forman in our union, and he turned out to be a media whiz.

Early on we got a lot of coverage from the local newspapers and TV stations. I did an interview for the City Pages, Minneapolis's weekly Villlage Voice rag, and they ran a lengthy and very favorable piece on us that a lot of my coworkers read. But Forman's big project was to get us national coverage. He wanted either the Wall Street Journal or the New York Times. I was rooting for the Times, because I'd had a Monday through Friday student rate subscription to it for 6 years. Forman of course came through. The Times was flying down a writer to do an interview, and Forman wanted me to talk to him. I was going to be in the Times!

The Wednesday of our interview I was working at Dinkytown with Micah Barley. Micah had just recently stepped up and become an integral committee member. He had organized a union shift-cover system so that when you were sick you could send out a text to find somebody to work for you. He was doing 1-on-1s and had collected signatures for our recognition petition. He wore a union button at work and distributed union literature. Whereas I was a loud-mouthed controversial union agitator, he was a calm universally respected voice of the union. And he was clearly bummed that he couldn't do the interview with the New York Times.

Well what the hell. I didn't want to do an interview if it was going to demoralize my fellow worker. No media coverage was worth damaging the union cause in our store. So I bullshitted and cajoled Micah and Emily into doing the interview in my stead. I told them I didn't give a shit about the media, and besides I was quitting after the election anyway and it was time for other workers to take on leadership roles. It worked. Micah and Emily were pumped.

I covered for Emily, who was working the night shift that day, and they went over to Tony's Diner and did their interview.

A few days later the Times flew down a photographer, and I made that into an organizing event too. Forman had him meet us at the store at shift change,

Union vote continues on D4 ▶

A Jimmy John's employee recently sported a button showing support for the Industrial Workers of the World.

and I got just about everyone from both the day and night shift to participate. Eight of us from the store posed out front on the sidewalk cracking jokes while this Times guy took hundreds of pictures. Then we dispersed and he took hundreds more pictures of just Emily and Micah.

Ultimately the story ran on the front page of the business section in the Times alongside a picture of Rob Mulligan and Steve Smith, a worker at the Skyway store downtown. It barely referenced the interview with Emily and Micah.

Which in my mind totally justified the way I'd dealt with the whole affair. The media's going to write the story the way they want to write it. Whatever they think will sell papers or attract viewers, that's the storyline they'll choose. What we say to them doesn't matter a whole lot, so we might as well use these media events to build support for the union.

I kept my nose down and continued doing 1-on-1s and collecting pictures and quotes for our posters. If we won the election, we'd get all the media we could handle. If not, we'd fade from the public view. That's how I saw it.

WE ARE THE UNION

"Because I have $20 to live off for 2 weeks every paycheck."
Gaby Gagnon, Stadium Village

"Because I can't afford my bills."
JJ Mangen, Block E

"Help the Union! Help yourself!"
Jesse Soderstrom, Stadium Village

"For all my coworkers who I've grown to love."
Von G. Berry, 9th St

"4 years without a raise."
Grant Richardson, Calhoun

"Hazard pay is a-okay!"
Alex Card, Dinkytown

"Because I made a better wage when I was 16 years old."
Matthias Sturn, Franklin

"United we stand, divided we fall!"
Ridge Larson, Knollwood/Stadium Village

"Our spirits need a lift and our workers need a raise."
Ayo Collins, 9th St

"Because we depend on these jobs for our livelihood and deserve a liveable wage."
BK Koppy, Dinkytown

"I will never feel pressured to deliver sandwiches during a tornado warning again."
Emily Przybylski, Dinkytown

"Because 3.5 million fast food workers could use a little inspiration." *Mike Wilklow, Dinkytown*

"Because they locked me out at 4am when we close and made me wait for the buses to start running in 40 below weather."
Ian MacDonell, Dinkytown

"Because I'm tired of seeing my coworkers mistreated for being sick."
Jaim'ee Bolte, 9th St

"Because people can't afford to take time off or go to the doctor when they're sick."
Erik Forman, West End

"To make history!"
David Boehnke, Skyway

"It's a step forward for minimum wage workers."
Anthony Janik, Dinkytown

"The Union is our Song!"
Dan Rude, 9th St

"To fuel a much-needed change."
Bob Hollister, Block E

"Because I can't feed my kids on minimum wage."
Jen Thompson, West End

"Cause I need more bread to keep the bread baking!"
Ben Yela, 9th St

"Because I don't get paid enough for this."
Mike Freeman, Knollwood

"Because I need money for school."
Callie Bensel, Dinkytown

"Cause I've never seen my bosses sweat at work."
Tim Roach, 9th St

"Because I'm 21 years old and want to be able to afford to act like I'm 21."
Jen Arbelius, Dinkytown

"Two years at minimum wage. That sucks."
Micah Buckles-Farley, Dinkytown

"Because we shouldn't have to be scared of the bosses."
Max Specktor, Block E

"To keep the man in check, push the status quo and try for a better life."
Austin Williams, Calhoun

"Any threat to labor is treason to America." - Abe Lincoln"
Dan Van Laeger, Calhoun

"Because I'd like to get paid a reasonable wage."
Kelsey Moses, Dinkytown

"It's just basic fairness. They treat people like numbers. We need to stand up for basic fairness!"
Cyrus Butler, Calhoun

"Because this will bring respect and a higher standard of living to the service industry."
Davis Ritsema, Calhoun

"Friends - let's end this corporate tyranny together!"
Nico Warsvan, Calhoun

"We need to join together, this union will improve our workplace."
Sam Dungan, Riverside

"For all the parents working hard for minimum wage to feed their kids."
Paulmer Johnson, Skyway

VOTE FOR YOUR COWORKERS.
VOTE FOR YOURSELF.
VOTE UNION OCTOBER 22nd!

Chapter 43
Diversity

October 3rd, 2010

Friday I went to the Captive Audience. Those meetings really fuck with me. I was very vocal and came off looking pretty good, but so did Mike Mulligan. Emily spoke up and called him out for giving a $2 raise to Steve at Skyway, which he denied.

October 20th, 2010

Gave Marly a ride back to the workhouse, which was a trip. 20 years old, 3 kids, another on the way, and he stays at the workhouse out in Plymouth. $3 bus rides both ways to work. And he's still voting NO. Probably.

Rare Vote Set On a Union In Fast Food

By STEVEN GREENHOUSE

MINNEAPOLIS — The Jimmy John's restaurants here are known for serving attitude with their sandwiches. Many of their young workers wear nose rings, beards and dreadlocks, and the shops sport mottoes like "The Customer Is Usually Right" and "Subs So Fast You'll Freak."

But recently, the employees at the 10 shops here have started to exude more attitude than management would like. Some of the

CRAIG LASSIG FOR THE NEW YORK TIMES

Rob Mulligan, left, whose father owns the Jimmy John's franchise outlets in Minneapolis, and Steven Smith, a worker.

When the New York Times article went to print, the picture they used for the cover page was of Rob Mulligan leaning on a counter with this guy Steve who worked at Skyway.

Steve was a sweet 40-year-old black man who had worked in the franchise for years. He was from L.A. and had spent several years in prison, during which time he'd given up drinking. A former boxer, the Mulligans had tried to get him to do security for late nights at the Block E store downtown.

Midnight to 3am shifts at a whopping $7.50 an hour. He quit doing it when they refused to pay him a decent wage.

David was our strongest organizer at the Skyway store and had been trying to get Steve involved in the union the entire time he'd worked there. At times I had heard Steve was coming to a meeting, but he always flaked and never came.

After we filed for the election, the Mulligans decided they wanted Steve on their side too. They gave him a $2 raise on the pretext of promoting him to "Slicer," a new position.

When we did our tip jar action, one of the Skyway managers took down a tip cup and David put it back on the counter. For violating the "no tip jar" rule, the Skyway GM Krysta gave written disciplinary warnings to not only David but also the other two workers on his sandwich line, including Steve. Steve got pissed at David for getting him in trouble.

This was all part of an organized effort by the owners and the union busters to court the black workers in our franchise and portray the union as a bunch of whiney white boys who cared more about our political agenda than the lives of our coworkers.

A bit of demographics on the workforce in our franchise:

At the time of the election we had about 200 workers across 10 stores. A slim majority of the workers were inshoppers and the rest were drivers.

Of the delivery drivers, 90% of us were white and 95% of us were male.

The inshop workers were about half black folks and half white folks, with just a few latino and asian workers. A slim majority of inshop workers were women.[90]

So in broad terms, we were majority white but a big 25% chunk of the workers were black. Two thirds men, one third

---

[90] These statistics are based off the Excelsior list of all eligible voters in the election and my memory of who was who. I give my memory a +/- 5% margin of error. I knew pretty much everybody in the eight Minneapolis stores but very few people in the two St. Louis Park stores.

women. But the two job classes — driver and inshop — had very different makeups.

Now a brief history of the dynamics of the JJWU:

When I started organizing I expected that inshoppers would form the core of our committee. Drivers made more money, which I figured would make them feel privileged and less likely to get involved. I could not have been more wrong.

For the entire four years I had been involved in the campaign, the core organizers had been mostly drivers. The number one reason: turnover.

The most common inshop shift at JJs was the lunch rush shift. It was typically around 4 hours long but was commonly as short as 2 hours. We had inshoppers making $20 a day and trying to pay their bills. It's hard to convince someone in that position to not take another job — any job — as soon as they find one.

The other big barrier we faced in trying to build a diverse committee boiled down to young inexperienced white organizers who lacked the confidence to set up 1-on-1s with black men and women from the hood. When those 1-on-1s did occur, often the white organizers tried to protect their black coworkers by not pushing them to take a visible public role in the campaign.

We were constantly discussing how to make the union more diverse. The ideas from those discussions that stuck with me the most came from Ayo — the most active black guy on our committee.

Ayo's advice was to not make a big deal out of race. If you try getting somebody involved in the union just because they're black and you want black people in the union, it's going to feel weird for both of you. If you're open and sincere with someone, skin color and gender won't matter.

We certainly tried, but with poor results. Several of the social leaders amongst the black inshoppers in the franchise became passive union supporters, but none of them ever took on tasks and became active committee members.

Once an anti-union campaign starts, anyone who isn't already active in the union becomes a target for the union busters.

The second week in October, district manager Jason Effertz drove around to all the stores and dropped off bags of anti-union buttons. Managers encouraged workers to wear them, with mixed results.

At Dinkytown the only person I ever saw wear an anti-union button was my coworker Marly. He was a 20-year-old black man and father of three who commuted from a work house in the suburbs and made minimum wage. Even though we had a very pro-union store with multiple capable organizers, none of us had ever done a 1-on-1 with Marly.

Before we went public as a union I saw the owner Mike Mulligan maybe twice a year. He mostly stayed in his lakeside resort out in Minnetrista and left the business to his son Rob. After we filed for an election he was everywhere, including inside our store at Dinkytown telling Marly how 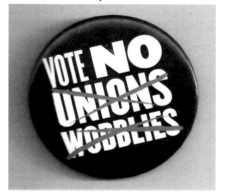 much he appreciated him. This is typical anti-union shit — the union busters come in and play bad cops while parading the owners around as the good cops. I can't say I know how Mike and Marly's conversations went, but it must have been enough to get Marly to wear that anti-union pin, which broke my heart.

I confronted Marly behind the store after that shift and asked him why he was wearing an anti-union pin. He tried to play it off like it wasn't a big deal. I told him it made me feel like he was siding with the owners against his coworkers and that it hurt me. He never wore an anti-union pin again, and I spent the next two weeks trying to get to know Marly better and having conversations that I should have had months earlier.

All in all I'd say the union busters' attempt to divide the workers in our franchise along race lines failed. Once the anti-union campaign kicked into gear, it quickly became clear that the strongest anti-union sentiment amongst non-management workers was going to come from white male delivery drivers.

One of the delivery drivers at the West End store in St. Louis Park created an anti-union Facebook page. I never knew him, but Forman assured me he was a jackass and didn't speak for anybody else in the store. At my store the only anti-union voice was Altan, an arrogant white delivery driver who didn't speak for anyone else in the store.

The most anti-union store in Minneapolis was the Skyway store downtown. It had a smaller staff because it was only open weekday days. It was also the most strikingly segregated store in the franchise. There were literally two black sandwich lines of 3 workers each, one white sandwich line, and then a white back area where the drivers in the store milled around between deliveries.

The 3 managers at Skyway were vehemently anti-union, as were 3 of the white male delivery drivers – Andy Germillion, Chris McCarthy, and Ben McCarthy.

The assistant manager Rene Nichols and the three anti-union drivers became the face of the anti-union campaign. They harassed union member David incessantly – Ben McCarthy would eventually get fired for bringing dog shit to work and putting it in David's coat pocket. Rene spent all her time at work complaining about David and trying to enforce nit-picky and arbitrary rules on him. For instance, she sent him home from work one day for leaning against a counter.

But those guys sucked anyway. Chris McCarthy I knew as the jackass who always tried to cheat on his girlfriend with Lita by offering to sell her weed[91]. Ben McCarthy was one of

---

[91] She repeatedly explained to him that she didn't smoke weed, but I guess that was his only pickup line. You may have forgotten Lita – she started our Poker Nights in 2009. She's also sleeping in my bed right now and I love her.

those suckups who in mandatory work meetings would get really enthusiastic about how everybody in the store needed to cover up their tattoos and upsell bacon. I figured we were lucky to have them as our anti-union campaign.

The five black inshoppers at Skyway mostly stayed out of the union arguments. David had been talking to them about the union for months but had failed to get anybody actively involved in committee work. Breon had come to the mass meeting but did not participate in the march on the boss the day we went public. Still, they didn't wear anti-union buttons and were quietly supportive of the union.

Chapter 44
Eyes on the Fries

October 16th, 2010

Let me at least outline the rest of my week before I forget.
Friday:

Ridiculous end to the night. Stix, Ayo, Lita, Lyric, Dan Rude's before that.

Used David's computer at his house to work on the poster, while him and a few others made picket signs.

1-on-1 with Kieran and Ryan Fox at Blarney's in Dinkytown. Fantastic!

1-on-1 with Margaret at Ginelli's. Free pizza, great talk.

Went into Skyway earlier and hung out across the counter from David for 5 minutes or so. Completely ignored Krysta who was sitting at a table.

Worked wasted at the Oak St. store, put on a hell of a performance. That's 1000 words in itself, but no time. Hard Times closes soon[92].

Dropped Lucius off at Nitali's. She said she'd take care of him for the next week. I don't have time for my dog right now.

Woke up at Micah's new house in Prospect Park.

---

[92] Hard Times closed at 4am. I was putting in long days.

Wasted testimony to NLRB agent about JJ's plan to pay people to vote on election day.

Fuck, no time. Even more briefly:

Thursday:

Most unions will not file for a union election until they get 75% of the workforce to sign the recognition petition, and even then they usually lose the election. We had filed a petition with 109 signatures, about 55% of the workforce.

The reason I felt confident in filing with such a slim majority was that I believed none of us had reached our peak potential in organizing. We had no paid organizers, so all the time and energy we put into the campaign outside of work was on a voluntary basis. It was easy to get tired, and there was nobody to force you back to setting up 1-on-1s if you weren't in the mood.

But with the election we were putting all our eggs in one basket. We had to win or the campaign would die. I expected the election would force us all to get off our asses and throw everything we had into organizing. I was right about that.

With two weeks until the election, our committee was on fire.

The Calhoun store had a strong shop committee of Davis, Joram, Dan Van, and Neko. They had met with all their coworkers and built overwhelming support for the union in their store.

Davis was also building relationships with outside supporters through our Solidarity Committee. A group of young women had become active in the Solidarity Committee, and one of these women organized an event at the University of Minnesota where they screened a short documentary called "Eyes on the Fries." The film discussed issues facing service and retail workers in the United States.

Emily and Ayo spoke at the event, and several of my coworkers attended. During the discussion session after the screening I spoke about the gains we'd already made. Raises for 30-40 people, a moratorium on bullshit firings, the right to refuse delivering in unsafe conditions. The women who organized the event would later go on to become wobblies and initiate organizing campaigns of their own.

At the Block E store our key union members were Max, Rikki, Jeff, and Bob. The franchise office where the union busters had set up shop was in the back of the Block E store, and there were constant confrontations. In one funny lapse of composure, LRI agent Rebecca Smith taunted Max by saying, "Well why don't you just go throw a Molotov cocktail at somebody" and then storming away. Block E had a higher percentage of pot smokers than any other store in the franchise and stayed pretty well-humored about the entire union campaign.

Max and I tabled for the union at a Propagandhi show. It was an all ages Triple Rock show packed with high school punk rockers. Max spoke on stage about the campaign. We received excellent reviews from that demographic.

At Riverside we had Travis, Jared, Sam, and Ben all advocating for the union. Travis was a detail-oriented sober non-smoker who lived in a filthy punk house. He was a new hire and ineligible to vote in the election but immediately became involved in committee work. He told me that one day Maurice, an older born-again black man with a teardrop tattoo I had befriended back when I worked at Riverside, had crumpled up an anti-union letter and thrown it at his manager's feet. That made me smile.

In the St. Louis Park stores Forman was doing 1-on-1s and had finally made good contacts. Mike F., a high schooler who worked at the Knollwood store, came out to the "Dance

Against Debt" event my comrades at the Dinkytown JJs had organized. It was a moving dance party that went from Riverside JJs to Dinkytown JJs and was intended to highlight the issues of high tuition and low wages. Or maybe they just wanted to dance. Anyway, Mike took photographs at the event and started working with our committee to meet up with Knollwood workers.

Mike B. from Knollwood was down too and started working on setting up benefit shows. We had tripled our number of Mikes!

Franklin was full of graffiti kids who smoked the dankest of doobies and were impossible to drag to meetings. Manuel and Matthias assured us that most of the workers in the store were down, but I worried nonetheless. In the weeks leading up to the election myself and others would swing by the store on the night shifts to drop off flyers and shoot the shit.

At Oak Street we were really at a disadvantage. The store hadn't even opened until after we went public and we hadn't had any time to build a strong shop committee. I was covering shifts and setting up 1-on-1s with the workers there, several of whom became strong union supporters. Ridge, Erica, Tiana, Zach, Gaby, Katie, and Jesse all gave pictures and quotes for our posters. But we didn't have a strong experienced organizer in the store, and we didn't have any time to develop one.

9th St. was one worker away from being 100% pro-union. Ayo, who had dropped out of our committee back in 2009, was back with a vengeance. He was speaking at events, writing union literature, and trying to convince his friends in the bike messenger scene to support the union. Besides him, Jaim'ee, Von, Dan Rude, and Stix were all wearing union pins and talking a big game.

At Skyway the union was getting our collective ass handed to us, but I've already discussed that.

All around town the JJWU was the word on the street. Sympathetic organizations had signs up in their windows exclaiming their support. We marched from Loring Park to Block

159

E waving picket signs and blaring dance music. The election was in all the newspapers, and you couldn't go anywhere without seeing somebody in a "Wages So Low You'll Freak" t-shirt.

Everyone on our committee was doing their part, and it was amazing.

I stayed focused on 1-on-1s. Always 1-on-1s. The basic unit of union organizing. Some days I had multiple formal 1-on-1s. Then I would go out drinking and meet up with more coworkers.

I became so busy with organizing work that I decided to find a dogsitter. A week before the election I dropped my furry confidant Lucius off with a friend. This was crunch time, and I wanted to give the campaign everything I had.

WE ARE THE UNION
UNITED FOR FAIR WAGES, GUARANTEED HOURS, RESPECT AND DIGNITY.

Hodan Abdi, Knollwood • Jen Arbelius, Dinkytown • Callie Bensel, Dinkytown • Von G. Berry, Riverside • Bartholemew Boeckenstedt, West End • David Boehnke, Skyway • Jaim'ee Bolte, 9th St • Matt Bongers, Dinkytown •Micah Buckley-Farley, Dinkytown • Cyrus Butler, Calhoun • Alex Card, Dinkytown • Todd Cole, Block E • Ayo Collins, 9th St • Emma Dahl, Calhoun • Jim Dolan, Knollwood • Sam Dungan, Riverside •

Moses, Dinkytown • Rikki Olsen, Block E • Emily Przybylski, Dinkytown • Ethan Rawlings, 9th St • Grant Richardson, Calhoun • Davis Ritsema, Calhoun • Tim Roach, 9th St • Demetris Robinsin, 9th St • Sarah Roen, West End • Dan Rude, 9th St • Carson Sandberg, Dinkytown • Danica Schwartz, 9th St • Jesse Soderstrom, Stadium Village • Max Specktor, Block E • Matthias Sturn, Franklin • Eric Swanson, 9th St • Forrest Thompson, West End •

Travis Erickson, Riverside • Erik Forman, West End • Mike Freeman, Knollwod • Gaby Gagnon, Stadium Village • Kanika Hatchet, Calhoun • Bob Hollister, Block E • Jared Ingebretzen, Riverside • Anthony Janik, Dinkytown • Paulmer Johnson, Skyway • BK Koppy, Dinkytown • Ridge Larson, Knollwood/Stadium Village • Manuel Levins-Holden, Franklin • Zack Lewis, Stadium Village • Jake Lindgren, Knollwood/Calhoun • Joram Livengood • Calhoun • Ian MacDonell, Dinkytown • JJ Mangen, Block E • Kelsey

Jen Thompson, Franklin • Sean Tobin, Riverside • Dan Van Laeger, Calhoun • Niko Waryan, Calhoun • Mike Wilklow, Dinkytown • Austin Williams, Calhoun • Craig Wyss, 9th St • Ben Yela, Riverside

VOTE FOR YOUR COWORKERS.
VOTE FOR YOURSELF.
VOTE UNION OCTOBER 22nd!

Chapter 45
Alcoholism

Wednesday October 20th, 2010

(illegible)
Just kidding. Still Tuesday.
That's how fucked up I am. At 12:30.
Well shit. Guess I can't drink any more tonight. But I ain't going home!

In case you haven't put the pieces together yet: I had a drinking problem.

In 4 years of working at Jimmy John's I had two completely sober weeks.

I kept my alarm clock across the room from my bed so that I would have to stand up to reach it. Five days a week I would be torn out of a deep drunken sleep by some awful blaring Christian pop music. I'd spring up and run across the room to make it stop. Then I'd spend ten minutes hunched over on a chair getting dressed, every muscle in my body hungover and screaming at me. I used to joke at work that I should get paid more because I was always hungover and I smoked, so logically I had to work harder.

My hangovers at work sometimes put me in an awful mood, but usually I was hilarious. I prank called the store while I was on deliveries. I played *Chorus Line* songs on the store stereo. I rang in "no ice" on sandwiches and other nonsense. In general my hangovers were a big hit.

In organizing you have to identify social centers where workers congregate outside of work. At Jimmy John's these were almost always bars or party houses. So that's where I hung out, and that's where I had the vast majority of my union conversations. I hung out with Riverside folks at Palmers. Dinkytown folks at Burrito Loco. Block E folks at Gang Chen. 9th St. folks at the Local. These are all bars.

After a certain point I began to view that as my role in the campaign. I was the drunk organizer. I was the guy who would go to any bar or any party where I could find JJ workers and advocate for the union. That was my strength. I would never back down from an argument and I could get into vicious debates without making people hate me. After all, I was just drunk.

In the weeks leading up to the election, my drinking hit a whole new level. Whereas before I had been primarily a late night drinker, that Fall I became a happy hour drunk. Almost every day after work I would go to Burrito Loco with Micah and Ryan and whoever else was working that day. Burrito Loco was an obnoxious college bar full of amateur drinkers and ridiculous drink specials, like $2 pitchers and 29 cent beers. Always 2 for 1s. We would stake out a table in the corner by the dartboard and order some wings, play some cribbage, talk some shop.

Ryan was my GM at Dinkytown, and I considered him the best manager in the franchise. He was great at all the non-human elements of his job, like keeping everything stocked and making sure we had enough ingredients prepped. He used a regular schedule, so we didn't have to worry about working different hours from week to week. He almost never fired anyone and would always advocate for the workers in our store. And he was my friend.

Ryan was following orders for the anti-union campaign. I don't know what all that entailed, but from what I gleaned it was mostly reporting people's opinions about the union to the owners. He identified the key organizers and our friends. The union busters acted on this information by dividing us in the captives and the Mulligans met with workers who Ryan told them were on the fence. We had expected all this and told Ryan to do what he had to do to keep his job. We were happy that the atmosphere in our store was chill, as opposed to some of the other stores where tensions between union supporters and management were running high.

It wasn't until a week before the election that Ryan and I had our first fight.

That Thursday at work Ryan was making a schedule for election day. Rob Mulligan had told him to schedule everybody who wasn't working on election day to come into work so the company could shuttle them to the polls. I had been expecting the company to pull some blatantly illegal shit in the final week, and to me this was it.

The legal term governing election day is called "laboratory conditions." It means that the day of a union election should be the same as any other work day. To schedule 25 workers for a shift that usually has 8 would be a clear breach of this law. I said as much to Ryan and he tried to argue it with me, saying that everybody should get a chance to vote. He said something about workers who didn't want the IWW to represent them and that's when I started yelling.

Why would any worker not want collective bargaining!? What could any of us possibly lose!? Everybody would get to vote down any contract they didn't like! Even fucking managers would get raises, because if inshoppers got raises then PICs would have to as well and it would have a trickle upward effect! This whole anti-union campaign was a bullshit deception by the owners to trick workers into accepting our shitty wages and our lack of any benefits whatsofuckingever! I was going to throw a fit about this shit with the labor board and we'd just see if it was legal or not!

Afterwards I felt like garbage. I didn't want to be fighting with Ryan. He was my friend, and besides he was the only GM in the franchise who was somewhat supportive of the union.

After Ryan finished his paperwork that day we got liquor and hung out behind the store with Micah. Ryan had a bottle of some nasty rum and we took it down pretty quickly. Then we went to Burrito Loco and got shitty drunk playing darts and beer pong. After that we went to the pedestrian bridge that goes over the train tracks in Dinkytown, where we drank beers and bonded in the twilight.

Ryan and I both apologized to each other and hugged. Ryan said he was actually rooting for the union but was caught in the middle between the owners and us. I said I know, that's

164

what happens when you're a manager. Or something like that. I actually don't remember all that well, because I was drunk off my ass.

Moments like that make it hard for me to say my alcoholism was bad for my organizing. My most emotional conversations usually came when my blood was boiling with booze, when I'd express feelings I kept locked up deep inside the rest of the time.

I know I didn't have to be drunk to organize. In fact, when I talk about 1-on-1s I always mean sober conversations. I tried to set up 1-on-1s during the day at coffee shops and diners. And I tried not to drink before I went to meetings.

But I had it in my head that I couldn't operate in groups of people unless I was drinking. And I couldn't open up to people unless I was drinking.

Probably that was just the booze making me think that, and maybe if I ever quit drinking I'll change my tune. But right now I'd have to say that I was a hell of a drunk organizer. The liquor was tough on my body, which was slowly breaking down. I was constantly battling depression, and alcohol probly didn't help with that either. But in the context of organizing, my drinking felt more like an asset than a barrier.

I did end up talking to the labor board about the Mulligans' plan to change the scheduling on election day. The following Monday when I came into work Ryan told me with a smile that Rob had called him in a panic and told him to schedule it just like a regular Friday. I guess I had been right.

Then the day before the election towards the end of my shift I saw Marly sitting at a table in the dining area. I had been trying to talk to him about the union for the past few weeks and figured this was my last chance for an 11th hour appeal. I walked up and sat down at his table. Ryan was the only other person in the store, and when he saw me approach Marly he went in the back office so we could talk in private. I appreciated that.

Chapter 46
Sabotage

October 20th, 2010

After the meeting I told Mike the union's not going to ruin his business, we're not about to negotiate ourselves out of jobs. He didn't know how to respond and walked away.

Covered a shift at Stadium Village, which was fireworks too.

Then had a 1-on-1 with Tiana at Hard Times, which went really well. She's interested in being on the negotiating team if we win.

Went to Blarney's with Ryan and Micah and apparently got blackout drunk.

From there I don't really know. I was at Hard Times at 12:30, and I was in bed with C------ at 8am when I woke up. I remember bits and pieces. Found a note on my computer chair that said "Bike on couch, bike lock at 3130 18th Ave."

By the week of the election the community events boards in all the stores were full of pro-union and anti-union flyers. Our best lit was our "We Are The Union" posters, but we also posted flyers for events and workers rights. The anti-union lit was all about how we were anarchists and commies who wanted to destroy business at Jimmy John's via "sabotage."

I had been covering shifts at the new Oak Street store and trying to make inroads with the workers there. At Oak Street I witnessed the sabotage scare in full effect.

The Tuesday before the election I was working a ridiculously over-staffed lunch shift at Oak Street when I got in a screaming match with the GM Alex. One of the union supporters in the store had apparently broken a bunch of anti-union buttons. Alex was running around the store screaming that it was sabotage.

I challenged him on it and asked in what world breaking a piece of propaganda is considered sabotage. He said that the buttons were store property and that made it sabotage. He also cited a recent incident at the store in which the hoses that connected the soda syrup to the soda station had been switched around, so that people trying to pour Diet Coke got Sprite instead. He blamed this "sabotage" on the union as well. I said it sounded like incompetence.

The third piece of Alex's sabotage argument was about Margaret's rotten food incident at the Calhoun store. He said that Margaret, acting on the union's orders, had deliberately broken the cooler so that the food would spoil. That was just too much. I blew up and told him exactly what had happened and that he should stop trying to pin responsibility on the union for everything that went wrong in the stores.

AND HERE IS WHY...

1. WOBBLIES BELIEVE EMPLOYERS ARE THE ENEMY. WE BELIEVE IN WORKING TOGETHER AS A TEAM.

2. WOBBLIES WANT TO ABOLISH CAPITALISM. WE'RE PROUD TO BE AMERICAN!

3. WOBBLIES USE DIRECT ACTION AND SABOTAGE. WE BELIEVE IN COOPERATION, RESPECT, AND TOLERANCE.

4. WOBBLIES TAKE YOUR MONEY TO FURTHER THEIR CAUSE. WE PROVIDE JOBS TO HELP FURTHER YOUR CAUSE.

5. WOBBLIES WANT "A NEW WORLD ARISING FROM THE ASHES OF THE OLD." WE MAKE SANDWICHES. NO, REALLY!

THE IWW (WOBBLIES) ARE...

We were standing in the middle of the kitchen area surrounded by workers and arguing for several minutes. After a while I felt like I wasn't working and should find something to do. But all the sandwich lines were full, there were no deliveries, and all the after lunch cleanup was already done. So after a short pause I started right back in on Alex, ridiculing him for his sabotage claims. It was bizarre. I was always a hard worker but at that store I guess the expectations were low and standing around arguing was acceptable.

A lot of folks at the Oak Street store were wearing anti-union buttons, about 8 people out of a staff of 25. We had just as many workers from Oak Street on the We Are The Union posters, but at least during the day shift the union supporters there didn't feel comfortable speaking up about it. I did my best.

I hopped on sandwich lines next to workers with anti-union buttons and asked them why they were wearing them. Nobody gave me a good reason, in most cases I think they just wore them because it was what their manager wanted.

The most vocal anti-union worker in the store was Tiffany, a black inshopper who had actually signed our recognition petition but had flipped sides around the time she was promoted to backup PIC. I confronted Tiffany and she flustered me by saying "This is not what Martin Luther King wanted."

I took it as a racial statement — she was saying the union was for white people and not black people — and at first I had no response. Then I thought about it. "Wait a minute, what are you talking about? Martin Luther King was assassinated while he was in Memphis to speak at a union rally! Of course he would have supported our union. Why don't you?" Tiffany later said I was cute and she would get a drink with me but she still was voting NO.

The final element of the anti-union campaign I'll leave you with is our last captive audience meeting before the election, where Mike Mulligan gave his teary-eyed life story. He wasn't born rich, you see. He had to work hard to make his money, and with hard work he had found success in the business world. Jimmy John's was a family venture. He had started the business so that he could bond with his son. It had been a trying but rewarding experience for him.

He told us that he wasn't wealthy and showed us some tax document to back up his claim. Nevermind that he owned an estate and 10 Jimmy John's stores worth millions of dollars. Motherfucker was on the Super Bowl committee. But according to him he was as middle class as the rest of us.

Then he went through all the demands we had listed on our initial recognition petition and tried to refute them one by one. He said he was personally offended that the union would accuse his company of racial discrimination and sexual harassment, and at that point I tried to interrupt him. He just kept going and I shut up so as not to seem immature. Our wages were competitive, the company couldn't afford health care, we didn't actually need breaks, and so on.

After he was done I spoke up and referenced the petition we'd done at Dinkytown about AM Jason who was racially discriminating against and sexually harassing our coworkers. We had told Rob about it and he had warned Jason but taken no further action.

How could they claim that they didn't know about this? How could they claim that they dealt responsibly with harassment and discrimination? Rob, who was also there, countered by saying that he had fired Jason. Then several of my coworkers chimed in - yeah, but you fired him for stealing money, not for harassment!

So that was the anti-union campaign. The union was a bunch of communists who wanted to ruin the business to further our radical political agenda. The owners were loving family men who cared about their employees and service to the community. The union busters were a nuisance and creating hostility in the stores, but if you voted against the union they'd go away and everything would return to normal.

Pretty typical but more effective than I would have guessed. I was still confident that we'd win the election, but I knew it wouldn't be a landslide.

"It's the only union that would even think about organizing fast food," said David.   who has been instrumental in the drive.

GLEN STUBBE • gstubbe@startribune.com

Election so rare you'll freak

October 20th, 2010
It looks like we're going to win the election, but it's way too close. I'm fucking terrified. I've never wanted anything more in my life. And I'm feeling a ton of responsibility for it, since I was so passionate about filing for it. Hot damn.

I'm at the 8th St. Grill downtown with Reuben drinking bloody marys. Reuben is my oldest friend at Jimmy John's - we were roommates when we first moved to Minneapolis 8 years ago. Reuben has a drinking problem and mental issues. As such, he has had a hard time finding jobs. He has worked at Jimmy John's longer than any other job, and now that he is about to have a baby he's terrified of getting fired. I tell him he doesn't have to be public about his support for the union and that I'll do my best to protect his job.

I'm at Rainbow Foods in the Quarry talking to Danika across the deli counter. Jimmy John's is just one of her three jobs. She works seven days a week at three different service/retail jobs, and she still can't save money. We discuss the benefits she receives at Rainbow and the differences between her Rainbow union – the UFCW – and the IWW. Nobody at JJs will have union dues deducted from their paychecks.

I am in Mike B. and Jimmy D.'s kitchen in South Minneapolis. I've never met them before. They're two of our few contacts at the Knollwood store, and nobody has been able to reach them lately. So I biked over and knocked on their door. They invited me inside and it's really not all that awkward. They tell me a bunch of high school kids work at Knollwood, and some of them support the union.

I'm driving Hodan to her home in Hopkins after a union meeting. Hodan is an Islamic high school student who works at the two St. Louis Park stores. I try talking her up about work but get the sense she's searching for the correct answers and not speaking openly. I'm worried that the meeting overwhelmed her. She says her coworker and fellow student Mike F. makes movies and has been working on a short film about the Jimmy John's Workers Union.

I'm at Hard Times talking to Gaby over coffee. Gaby's a South High alum who's friends with a bunch of my roommates. She's loud and candid and cracks me up at parties. She works inshop at the new Oak Street store and is constantly broke. She supports the union but is hesitant to take on a larger role in the campaign.

I'm at Palmers getting a bloody mary with Paulmer from the Skyway store. He's excited about the union and says it's about time somebody stuck up for the little guy. He's also friends with all the anti-union folks at Skyway and it's strange to hear him talk about it. He says he just thinks they're misguided but are still good people. I don't give them that much credit.

I'm at Tony's Diner eating crappy Tony's food with Jesse. Jesse's actually my roommate and I'm in his room playing FIFA on his Playstation 3 all the time, but I wanted to have a formal 1-on-1 with him anyway. He's been delivering at Oak Street and is getting fed up with the overstaffing. Sometimes he gets cut an hour or less into his shift, and the only times he makes any money is when other people get cut or when he covers shifts at other stores. He says the night shifts are chill but day shifts are full of anti-union asskissers.

I'm with Ridge at Stub and Herbs. He's drinking a pint before he goes to work at Oak St. Pretty funny guy, he occasionally interrupts himself and says "I like beer," as if explaining his quirks. He says he was raised pro-union and he'll do whatever he can to help the campaign. Later he will smash a bunch of anti-union buttons and be labeled our lead saboteur.

I'm with Kelsey and a couple of her friends drinking an awful bloody mary at Blarney's. Kelsey only works a couple shifts a week at Dinkytown and is a terrible employee. She's worried that if she publicly supports the union the company will start caring when she no-call-no-shows. I don't know what to say to that, so I focus on why the union is righteous. She gives a picture and quote for the poster, then some other college student shows up and it turns into a meeting about a scene Kelsey will be acting in for a student film.

I'm at the Nomad World Pub after a Propagandhi show with Max, hanging out with some of his Block E coworkers. I'm all drunk and I confront Cip and JD about why they won't support the union. They say they don't want to talk about it. Choice line of mine — "You don't walk to talk about it cause you don't got shit to say!" Probly not the best way to advocate for the union.

172

I'm playing chess at Stub and Herbs with Zach. He used to work at Starbucks and has had experiences with the Starbucks Workers Union. Forman says he was never really down, but he's into the JJWU now and wants to find ways to get more involved. I tell him all our various meeting times and proceed to wallop him at chess.

I'm with Rachel at 5 Guys getting burgers. Rachel is tight friends with all the union members at Dinkytown but for some reason nobody has ever asked her to get involved. I remember meeting with her and Callie and TJ about the petition against AM Jason back in the day, but I guess we never followed up with her. Whoops. Rachel says she really hopes the union wins the election and so does her mom.

I'm at Ginelli's Pizza downtown meeting up with Margaret. I used to work here and they still give me free pizza. Margaret's working at Skyway now and is really frustrated with her coworkers. She feels terrible for David and says he doesn't deserve the harassment he receives. She's nervous about being on the poster because she thinks her coworkers will come after her too, but she lets me take her picture anyway and feels good about it afterward.

I'm at Hard Times with Tiana getting coffee. She works at Oak St. and is one of the few lady delivery drivers in the franchise. She has dread locks and a great sense of humor. I try to talk her into taking on more responsibility with the campaign and she's receptive but says our Sunday meetings conflict with her Grease Pit meetings. I tell her that when we win the election each store will need to elect a negotiator, and she says she would like to be that person at Oak St.

I'm at Hard Times drinking coffee with Erica. Also a lady delivery driver at Oak St. She's younger than me but has been a Hard Times regular as long as I have. I didn't know she worked at JJs until I ran into her at 1419 the other day. I think I hit on her once a while back and now I wish I hadn't.

She doesn't seem to hold it against me and is pretty pumped about the union. She hates the corporatism of JJs though and wants to quit. She says she'll wait to quit until she gets a chance to cast her vote.

I'm with Micah knocking on Crystal from Oak St.'s apartment door. It's two days to the election and Forman is spearheading a last ditch effort to go door-knocking and talk to all the workers in the franchise we haven't yet approached. Micah and I don't really know what we're doing and this house visit goes horribly. Crystal is so offended that we showed up unannounced at her door that she decides to stay in town to vote against the union. She had been planning on leaving town, apparently.

It's the night before the election and I'm playing the pre-election union party at the Paper Moose in Northeast Minneapolis. I dedicate Terracide's song "The Crew" to Erik Forman and say that he's been an inspiration to me. Somebody asks where he is. Where do you think? Out organizing!
Later I'm outside smoking and sending texts to Ryan Fox. I met with him a few nights ago at Blarney's and he said he was voting for the union but now he's freaking out. His last text is "Okay I get it!" I feel relieved and confident he's voting for the union.
The party is great. Mike B. from Knollwood set it up and it's all bands of JJ workers. At least 2 workers from every store are here, including all my best friends. Ayo, Micah, Emily, Max, Stix, and the list goes on and on. I brought my alarm clock and I'm going to crash here tonight. Then tomorrow morning I will bike to Block E, where I will act as the union's observer on election day.
Holy shit. We made it. It's finally happening.

It's the day before the election and I'm sitting at a table in the Dinkytown JJs dining area with my coworker Marly. He says he still hasn't made up his mind about voting. I look him in the eyes and tell him that the only ones who will know what he votes are himself and whatever God he believes in, so he should vote whatever he thinks is right.

WE ARE THE UNION
UNITED FOR FAIR WAGES, GUARANTEED HOURS, RESPECT AND DIGNITY.

Hodan Abdi, Knollwood • Jen Arbelius, Dinkytown • Mike Baillie, Knollwood • Nick Bates, Riverside • Callie Bensel, Dinkytown • Von G. Berry, Riverside • Bartholemew Boeckenstedt, West End • David Boehnke, Skyway • Jaim'ee Bolte, 9th St • Matt Bongers, Dinkytown • Margaret Brickley, Skyway • Micah Buckley-Farley, Dinkytown • Cyrus Butler, Calhoun • Alex Card, Dinkytown • Amy Champagne, Riverside • Todd Cole, Block E • Ayo Collins, 9th St • Emma Dahl, Calhoun • Jim Dolan, Knollwood • Sam Dungan, Riverside • Travis Erickson, Riverside • Erik Forman, West End • Mike Freeman, Knollwood • Gaby Gagnon,

Jake Lindgren, Knollwood/Calhoun • Joram Livengood • Calhoun • Ian MacDonell, Dinkytown • JJ Mangen, Block E • Kelsey Moses, Dinkytown • Rikki Olsen, Block E • Emily Przybylski, Dinkytown • Ethan Rawlings, 9th St • Grant Richardson, Calhoun • Greg Rick, Franklin • Davis Ritsema, Calhoun • Tim Roach, 9th St • Demetris Robinsin, 9th St • Sarah Roen, West End • Andrew Rogalski, Stadium Village/Dinkytown • Dan Rude, 9th St • Carson Sandberg, Dinkytown • Danica Schwartz, 9th St • Jesse Soderstrom,

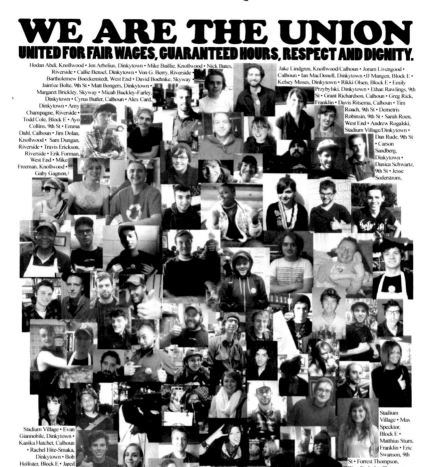

Stadium Village • Evan Giannobile, Dinkytown • Kanika Hatchet, Calhoun • Rachel Hite-Smaka, Dinkytown • Bob Hollister, Block E • Jared Ingebretzen, Riverside • Anthony Janik, Dinkytown • Erica Johnson, Stadium Village • Paulmer Johnson, Skyway • Tiana Johnson, Stadium Village • BK Koppy, Dinkytown • Ridge Larson, Knollwood/Stadium Village • Manuel Levins-Holden, Franklin • VillageZack Lewis, Stadium Village • Katie Lien, Dinkytown •

Stadium Village • Max Specktor, Block E • Matthias Sturn, Franklin • Eric Swanson, 9th St • Forrest Thompson, West End • Jen Thompson, Franklin • Sean Tobin, Riverside • Dan Van Laeger, Calhoun • Ryan Waage, Riverside • Niko Waryan, Calhoun • Mike Wilklow, Dinkytown • Austin Williams, Calhoun • Craig Wyss, 9th St • Ben Yela, Riverside

VOTE FOR YOUR COWORKERS. VOTE FOR YOURSELF.
VOTE YES.
OCTOBER 22nd. POLLING PLACES at BLOCK E and WEST END.

175

Chapter 48
Election Day

It's 8:30am and I'm biking down Central Avenue towards downtown. I barely slept but I'm full of adrenaline. The cool air helps to wake me. I stop and buy a newspaper out of a sidewalk box. We got our election in before winter, but just barely. In another month the city will be covered in ice and cyclists all over town will be deciding between skinny tires and knobbies.

I'm the first one to the Block E polling place. Block E is a failed downtown development project that was once filled with corporate chains but is now nearly vacant. We'll be voting in an empty Hooters on the second floor.

The other polling place is in St. Louis Park, and Forman is our observer there. I bet he's going to be bored out of his mind. Most of the voting will be here in Minneapolis.

The company entourage arrives before the Labor Board agents. Mike Mulligan, Rob Mulligan, their lawyer, and their rat – Steve. I'm polite and say hello but give Steve a cold hard glare.

After a few minutes the board agents arrive with their suits and briefcases. One's a middle-aged man and one's an attractive younger woman. They mingle with the Mulligans and their lawyer and then give Steve and me a page of observer instructions.

Yeah, this is definitely their game and not ours. Safe, controlled, bureaucratic. Dirty workers unsure what to expect and perfumed government agents telling them what to do. At least I get to be there.

Our committee originally wanted Von to be the Block E observer, probly for the same reason the company picked Steve and Tiffany - tokenizing. They're black. They're inshoppers. They're more stereotypically sympathetic.

But I was passionate about my desire for the role. I'd worked at all ten stores and knew more workers than anybody else in the franchise. I wanted the opportunity to look everybody in the eyes before they cast their vote. Maybe it was a mistake and I was being selfish. Too late to worry about that now. The union had voted for me.

When the polls open we're seated at a long table. The middle-aged suit on one end, then the young suit, then Steve, then me.

For the first half hour nothing much happens. Steve and the board agents make awkward small talk about the weather. They predict when people will come in to vote, what turnout will be like, etc. I offer very little input and start in on my crossword.

Soon workers start to arrive. It's mostly the downtown folks on their way to work. Seeing my friends peps me up and I start talking more. Steve asks for the Metro section of the paper and we begin to chat. Out of force of habit I ask him about work.

Steve says he's worked at JJs for years and bounced around between the downtown stores. I ask him about his experience as a de facto bouncer at Block E and he tells me about how crazy it gets on the weekends there. We discuss SK getting body-slammed at work by a drunk clubber and breaking his collarbone. We seem to agree on most things and it's hard not to like him.

Emily comes in and she's full of union energy. Ashley, the PIC at Block E, points at her anti-union button and says "I think you know what *I'm* voting." Riverside Derek and Dinkytown Derek. Max Spektor and Max Gable. Reuben takes way too long in the voting box and I get a queasy feeling. I wish I would have met up with him in these past couple weeks, but he'd lost his phone.

I ask Steve why he's observing for the company and he says because they asked him. The way he puts it they said they needed somebody to make sure the vote was fair and why would he reject that?

We discuss our experiences with the union. Steve talks about the Skyway store and how polarized it has become. He says he loves and respects David but believes David can push people away by always thinking he's right. I stand up for David

177

and say the problem is cowardly workers following the lead of company stooges.

The afternoon voting is way more tense for me. All I can think about is the union supporters who haven't voted yet. Where's Callie? Where's Tiana? Steve says he sees more pro-union people voting than anti-union and he thinks we'll win. But I'm pretty sure we're going to get whooped in St. Louis Park and need to win Minneapolis by a large margin. Where's Stix? Where's Ryan Fox?

To pass the time I talk with Steve. I've abandoned my crossword. We talk about where we're from and our experiences. He tells me about the violence he grew up around and why he quit drinking. I tell him about growing up in the sticks and living in a trailer park.

In the last half hour a bunch of union supporters arrive and I relax a little. There's Stix, sweaty and on a delivery for his courier job. Callie, Rachel, and Jen who had a hard time finding the empty Hooters. The only people I'm disappointed I don't see are Ryan Fox a couple others. I'm pretty sure we've won.

Right before the polls close Steve tells me that he voted for the union. That seems like a fitting end to my organizing career if I do end up quitting. One last 1-on-1, with the company observer at the polling site.

After the voting we have to wait for the board agents from the other polling place. In the meantime JJ workers and supporters begin descending on Block E en masse to witness the vote count. I'm outside smoking with Ayo and Davis and Emily and a bunch of other friends. I tell them I think it's going to be close but I think we have it.

When the count starts we're all crowded into the empty Hooters. A hundred union supporters, eight union busters, and the four board agents. The agents ask for a union observer to verify the count and somebody nominates me. "Screw that I've been sitting here all day! Somebody else do it!" People laugh and Jaim'ee volunteers.

First they go through the contested ballots. The only two the company and us don't agree on are both union votes. Karina, who was fired a month before the election but has a ULP pending. Katie, who was hired long enough ago to make her eligible but didn't work her first shift until after the cutoff date. Those votes are set aside. We'll see if they matter.

One of the board agents dumps all the ballots onto a table and starts pulling them out one by one. NO. YES. NO. NO. YES. NO. NO. NO.

Early on it's clear to everyone that we're getting our ass kicked. Except for the board agent grabbing ballots and shouting out votes, the rest of the room is still as death. I have a scrap of paper and a pen and am furiously tallying votes as the count proceeds. My heart is in my throat. When the NO count reaches 50, the agent stops and checks with the observers. They both have the NO count at 50. I have the YES count at 31.

After that we start to catch up. YES. YES. YES. NO. YES. NO. YES. YES. YES.

One ballot is contentious. The worker initially marked YES but then scratched it out and marked NO. I'm sure it's Reuben's. He took way too long in the box. There's some debate but the agent rules that the intent is clear and records it NO. I'd have to agree.

YES. NO. YES. NO. NO. YES. YES.

When the YES count reaches 50 the agent pauses again to verify with the observers. They both have 50 too. I have the NO count at 60.

YES. YES. YES. NO. YES. NO. YES. YES.

We're still closing the gap. I bet the St. Louis Park ballots were all together on top and he counted those first. I figured we'd lose there, but we dominated in Minneapolis. We're going to make it, I know it.

NO. YES. YES. YES. NO. YES. YES.

Finally there are only two ballots left and we've tied it! 85 to 85. The agent has been flying through the ballots but he pauses before these last two. It's so quiet you can hear your own breath.

179

NO.
NO.

There's a gasp in the room but I'm already moving forward towards the table. They have to recount it! Any vote that close you have to recount! We didn't lose! I won't believe it!

The board agent is clearly annoyed by me but he relents and goes through the whole thing all over again. It's even more painful the second time. The company men are in the corner congratulating each other and everybody knows how it's going to end. My initial denial is fading and I can feel the tears rising.

Then it's over and everybody's hugging and crying. I can hear Forman in my ear telling me not to sign something, that we're going to contest the results, that the company did so many illegal things something or other but I'm barely there.

I just want to get away. People are hugging me as I work my way towards the door.

Then I'm outside and I'm trying to smoke but I'm crying. I'm hugging Jaim'ee and we're crying.

Then I'm on my bike and I'm leaving. I pass by Steve and he stops me to ask if I'm okay.

No, I'm not.

October 23rd, 2010

We lost in heartbreaking fashion.

We will appeal on various counts of ULPs, and I guess I have no idea how that will go. I'm pessimistic. Potentially they could hold another election. I guess I don't know how that would go either. I'm pessimistic.

I feel like I let a lot of people down. All my old IWW friends thought this was a bad idea, an unwinnable strategy. But I convinced a bunch of 20-year-olds that we could do it. And broke all their hearts.

I know nobody's mad at me, but I can't help but blame myself. This was my dream.

I was still crying on my way to work today. Altan was already there for me. So I didn't have to work today.

I don't remember passing out last night. I do remember waking up at 6am and bawling my eyes out, trying to smoke a cigarette.

Wil had talked then biked my drunk ass home. I remember hanging out on the porch a bit. Two notables-

Ayo – "You told me on this porch that the hardest part of this campaign was watching Wil lose hope. Don't do that to me."

I also yelled "No" or something at David when he said he was going to talk to Steve about his voting yes.

Drinking on the stairs to nowhere on the West Bank with Wil before that. Palmers before that. Crying in front of Starbucks downtown before that. Before that, the count.

It was just like you see in the movies. A shitload of union supporters and a handful of company men watching a board agent count the ballots. Just remember losing big early in the count, then edging closer and closer till we finally tied at 85. And even then I believed. I was wrong.

I made them recount it, which was probly unnecessary. But it was so close. After that I don't remember. Some hugs, but I just wanted to get the fuck out of there. The guilt's unbearable.

I'm at BIG 10 bar and restaurant right now, hungover as shit and drinking water. There's thousands of people standing in line across the street, all down Washington Avenue. Maybe it's midterm election day. Nope, nevermind, Obama's speaking on the mall. I faintly remember hearing that.

Life goes on.

They're going to try to get me to keep fighting, but I'm so deflated and defeated right now I can barely stand. I went 4 years without crying and now it seems that's all I know how to do.

What do I do now?

Chapter 49
Aftermath

December 12th, 2010

Jumped off my roof drunk last night and now I have plantar fasciitis in my right foot. Think I'm gonna skip the meeting tonight.

Yesterday and Friday we had the worst blizzard since Halloween '91. About 2 feet of snow in 30 hours. Work yesterday was kinda fun. The streets were insane. I was driving with Emily and Bongers. Jordan was PIC. Nobody else made it in. 50mph winds. We closed early at 3pm. So did all the other stores. Drivers were refusing deliveries all across the franchise. Would have been a good night for a food service general strike.

Friday night I went with Noah to Margaret Brickley's party, which was awful. Everyone from Skyway JJs who sucks, plus Margaret and Dan Van. Then we biked through the beginning of the blizzard to Medusa, which was super fun. Varix played the best set I've seen since Frozen Teens at the Hexagon maybe 6 months ago. They're super-inspiring.

Earlier that day I recorded my guitar tracks for the new Terracide recording, and that went really well. Probly why I was in such a good mood. I'm thinking maybe I should focus on getting my artistic projects back on track – work on Terracide shit more and start writing again.

I feel like I'm going in a different direction than the rest of the committee. Seems the main concern of the committee right now is pushing this "10 Point Program" that I consider more-or-less useless. My focus has been on shop grievances and maintaining a union presence at Dinkytown. On the one hand I'm out of touch with our general strategy, but on the other hand ⅔ our active committee is coming out of Dinkytown. So I think my approach is right, at least for the winter.

But, I also want to move on with life. Specifically I want to go back to school and get a degree in Computer Science. I *would be researching my financial options right now, but Casey still hasn't paid the goddamn internet bill.*

Started working on a petition over hours cuts at Dinkytown. Basically a list of people who got their hours cut recently and would like to be offered shifts at other stores as they open up. Needs some work.

Yeah, I'm definitely skipping the meeting tonight. Just too depressed. But also I have nothing to do instead. Drunk drive home from Palmers? Maybe I'll just read. That's definitely cheaper.

The Metrodome collapsed during the blizzard.

The night of the election there was a party at my house. Friends have told me it was the most emotional night of solidarity they'd ever experienced. Everyone drinking together, crying together, singing together. I barely remember it, because I blacked out and crashed early.

The night after the election I do remember. Terracide played Von's birthday party at his house on 32nd and Cedar. I was extremely depressed and probly said two words during our whole set[93]. The highlight of the party was Erik Forman confronting Rene Nichols in the backyard. She and her sister Tonya had been two of the most vocal anti-union JJ managers.

Forman asked Rene if she thought she could shit all over JJ workers in the hopes of a promotion and then expect to be welcome at our parties. Her boyfriend shoved Erik, so Erik sucker punched him. It made the papers, and I remember telling everyone how I wished every stupid fight I saw at a party showed up in the Star Tribune.

Forman acknowledged Friday that he threw a punch, but said he only did so after he was pushed three times. "It's not relevant," he said. "It happened after the election. Besides, I weigh 120 pounds. I'm not intimidating to anybody."

---

[93] Besides the thousands of words of lyrics, of course. Terracide was nothing if not verbose. *Pyschotic pest nest in a chest against her breast. The rebels have risen they'll visit the prison tonight.* Stuff like that.

The meeting that Sunday was the most powerful meeting I'd ever attended. About 30 JJ workers sitting shoulder to shoulder in David's living room. We did a go-around where everybody talked about what they thought the union should do next. Everyone wanted to challenge the election results, and most people spoke about continuing to organize around our core issues. I said that I felt like I'd let a lot of people down.

In the weeks and months following the election, the union began focusing on more positive community events and job actions. We set up a series of concerts called Jimmy Jams that featured bands with JJ workers. We started doing monthly community meals that were popular and well-attended. Right before Christmas we did a holiday pay action where we had people in Santa hats stand outside the stores and ask customers to sign Christmas cards. The cards were addressed to the Mulligans and asked them to pay us time and a half on Christmas Eve.

Another moment that sticks out to me was when we distributed a letter that Ayo had written. It was one page with a picture of him at the top and a two paragraph testimonial about his involvement in the union. Everybody at Dinkytown appreciated that letter, even Altan.

In general though we were losing momentum. The excitement of the election was fading. The union busters had left and all the propaganda had come down from the community boards. Fewer and fewer people were wearing buttons either pro or against the union. Union subcommittees folded, and our Sunday meeting attendance settled back down to an average of about eight people a week.

Work started to feel like work again. Squeezing mayo into bins. Slicing cheese. Bagging deliveries. Washing dishes. Fighting the wind on Kasota Avenue for a $2 tip. Same old shit.

I became less and less involved in the committee. I still attended meetings but wasn't willing to take on tasks. The union decided to start pushing a "10 Point Program" similar to the list of demands we had circulated with our recognition petition, and I abstained from the entire project. I didn't see the point in circulating another petition if we weren't going to file for another election.

Still I continued agitating at the Dinkytown JJs and trying to organize shop actions. I guess I'd been organizing so long I didn't know how to stop. I talked to people about raises they were due. When we all got our hours cut for the holiday break at the university, I wrote up a petition and began circulating it to workers who wanted more hours.

Dealing with the Labor Board was a drag. Workers and managers all had to go down to the Labor Board office and give affidavits about the company's behavior preceding the election. I told them how 8 people received raises at Dinkytown the month after we went public, and how in 4 years at Jimmy John's I'd never seen that many people at one store get raises in a month. I spoke about Oak Street GM Alex running around the store screaming sabotage.

But none of it really mattered. All the Labor Board

Bribes, threats, punches alleged in unionization effort at Jimmy John's

● A week after losing a union election, the IWW accuses a Jimmy John's franchise owner of intimidation.

By CHRIS SERRES
cserres@startribune.com

A unionization drive at 10 Jimmy John's sandwich shops in the Twin Cities has turned decidedly ugly, with accusations of threats, bribery and even physical assault flying between union members and a local franchise owner.

A week after narrowly losing a rare union

election at a fast-food chain, the Industrial Workers of the World (IWW) accused local Jimmy John's franchise owner Mike Mulligan of waging a campaign to intimidate workers, making a fair vote impossible.

The union alleged in a 12-page petition filed Friday with the National Labor Relations Board that Mulligan's firm, Miklin Enterprises Inc., fired workers who openly supported the union, instituted a wage freeze, and offered bribes to workers in the weeks

Jimmy John's continues on D4 ►
SEE the workers' petition at Startribune.com

GLEN STUBBE · gstubbe@startribune.com
One of the Twin Cities Jimmy John's sandwich shops at which workers recently lost a close vote on whether to unionize. The union is asking the NLRB to nullify results of the election.

could do was throw out the election results, and then we could have another one. Whoop-de-doo. If we waited a year we could file another election anyway, so what exactly did we have to gain?

In the meantime I was getting into arguments with Ryan about his behavior during the election. He thought people deserved the raises he'd given them. So did I. But it was still a change from the status quo which made it an Unfair Labor Practice. Those were arguments I didn't want to be having. They had nothing to do with empowering workers or improving working conditions and everything to do with some useless court case. Bleh.

Overall I was burnt out and ready to leave Jimmy John's. I felt like I'd put in my time. But I found it hard to quit. I could probably find some other crappy delivery job. But I had all these tight friends in the JJWU that I didn't want to let down. Turns out I never had to make that decision.

It was the day after New Year's and I was biking back from a delivery on SE Cole. The streets were covered with a thin layer of powdery snow, and the snow was still floating down. The lunch rush had ended and the store was quiet, so I wasn't in much of a hurry.

I rolled up to the 4-way stop at 22nd and Como and checked for cars. I saw a vehicle approaching from my left but the intersection was clear. As I started to make my left turn I saw out of the corner of my eye that the Eastbound car was not slowing down.

Bike delivery folks make life-altering split decisions all the time. It happens so fast it feels instantaneous. In the time it takes to wink your eye I decided that I was not going to be able to clear the intersection. I had just started rolling and on the snow I couldn't accelerate fast enough. I was already leaning left so I tried to swing it all the way around and do a 180 to get out of the intersection back the way I had entered it.

I never heard brakes squeal, but I was told by witnesses that as the driver reached the STOP sign she finally applied her brakes. Didn't swerve though. I had almost cleared the intersection but didn't quite make it. From what I understand we collided head-on, my knee slamming into her passenger side fender. I flew up in the air and landed on my head[94].

It took me a minute or two to peel myself off the pavement. People were telling me to stay down, but I didn't listen to them. I stood up and started hopping around. The

---

[94] I was wearing a helmet. I always said that if I was gonna get killed riding my bike, it would be on my own time.

driver was out of her car and panicking. I just cursed. Motherfucking sonofabitch! Ow!

I could hop around but I couldn't bend my knee. Turned out my kneecap was shattered. Multiple fractures that would require multiple surgeries. My sandwich delivery days were over.

And just like that, I was out.

*

Conclusions

Losing that election is going to haunt me until the day I die. It was ours to win, and we lost by the narrowest possible margin. In basketball it would be like trailing by 1 with 0.1 seconds on the clock and missing the two free throws that would have won you the championship[95].

If we had won, this story would have a different ending. We would have held elections for union negotiators in all the stores. Steve who had been the company observer would now have been sitting on the other side of the table saying what he thought was fair for the workers. And if the company didn't negotiate in good faith we would have had enough momentum and organization to call for franchise-wide work stoppages. That's what I saw.

So why did we lose?

My gut answer will always be because I didn't do that last 1-on-1. I should have found Reuben in those last two weeks. I should have talked to Ryan Fox in person instead of texting him the night before the election. I shouldn't have fucked up that house visit with Crystal. I should have covered shifts in St. Louis Park. I should have done more.

I think it's the same for all our best organizers.

At the St. Louis Park polling site, two union supporters showed up to vote 5 minutes after the polls closed.

Damien from Calhoun never made it to the polls. Tory from Franklin. And one vote would have changed everything.

Another obvious answer is that we lost because of illegal union busting. That's the theory the Labor Board accepted.

---

[95] I've resisted sports analogies for 55,000 words. At least let me have one.

The union's objection to the election cited 21 allegations of misconduct by the company. They threatened a wage freeze. They threatened to eliminate bike delivery. They accused us of sabotage. They interrogated workers about their union activity. They took down union posters. In general they broke a majority of the laws that govern union elections.

The Labor Board found merit with enough of our allegations to take the case, and in January 2011 the company and the union reached an agreement to set aside the election results. The company did not have to admit any wrongdoing, and in return we had a year to ask for another election and would not have to submit a new recognition petition.

At that point though the union didn't want another election. I did, but I was out of work and on my way out of the campaign. Most of our active committee was opposed to elections in the first place. And it was the middle of winter. And if you're going to have another election you might as well circulate another petition anyway. You can't win an election without talking to all the workers.

Basically what we won with that court case was the right to say that, legally speaking, we never lost a union election. Practically speaking though, we still lost.

Concerning the union's strategic decisions we made throughout the course of the campaign, I can't pinpoint any that in retrospect I consider major mistakes.

Wobblies all across the IWW have had problems with our dual membership structure. Membership in the JJWU was informal. You just had to become active in the campaign and call yourself a member. Membership in the IWW was formal. You had to pay union dues and sing wobbly songs. So workers could be members of the JJWU without being members of the IWW.

I can see how that's problematic, but I haven't heard a better idea yet. Were we supposed to make our coworkers pay to attend their first union meeting? Or were we supposed to tell all the workers who participated in our actions and attended meetings that they weren't part of the union and really the union was just the 12 JJ workers who paid dues to the IWW?

I'm sure there's a better way to handle membership in a union where dues check-off is unconstitutional, but until I see it I'll have to say we did the best we could given the circumstances.

The other major strategic point I've questioned is our relationship to middle management. Specifically I've wondered if we should have given managers with whom we had good relationships a role in the union.

On the one hand, that's illegal anyway. Supervisors cannot legally involve themselves in unions. Then it becomes an employer-run organization, according to the law.

But fuck the law.

The bigger problem is that organizing is about empowering workers to stand up to their managers and how are you going to do that when their manager is at the union meeting? That's why I didn't want managers involved.

Still, at the time of the election I had two good friends who were general managers in the franchise. I'd worked with both of them prior to their promotions, and I trusted both of them. Their jobs sucked too, believe me. And since the election, both of them have told me that if the union would have approached them they could have tipped the election in our favor. There may be something to that.

At the end of the day I'd say my gut answer to why we lost the election is closer to the truth than any of the legal arguments or academic analyses. Really we were just two workers short.

Companies will always break the law during union elections. Why wouldn't they? They have nothing to lose. To me that's not an excuse, it's just a given. We knew that and we filed for an election anyway.

And the problem wasn't any lapse of judgment on the part of the JJWU. During my involvement in the campaign I worked with some of the brightest and most righteous people

I've ever met. We didn't get everything right but we never did anything overly shady or inane.

It was just a matter of inexperience. We did our best but we were all learning as went. We needed one more committee member. Two more 1-on-1s. And we came up short. That's why we lost the election.

*

While I was walking around on crutches and living off Worker's Comp I debated what I would do when I returned to work. Specifically I was considering a big push for a redo election.

I wanted desperately out of the campaign. For years I had lived a high turnover life. Always meeting new workers. Always meeting new people at parties. New roommates. New lovers. I was fried. I wanted quiet. I didn't need any more friends. I wanted to stop losing track of the friends I already had.

But I also hated losing. We had come so close in that election and we had learned so much. Maybe one more try and we could win it. Course I'd have to convince everybody all over again.

I never had to make that decision, because Jimmy John's fired me before the doctors cleared me to go back to work.

In my absence the union had decided to focus on organizing around sick days. We made "Sick of Working Sick" buttons and workers in all the stores started wearing them.

We marched into the franchise office and met with Rob Mulligan to discuss the issue of working sick. How people were disciplined and occasionally fired for missing shifts due to sickness. How workers couldn't afford to miss shifts and ended up preparing food while they were still contagious. We told him that if the company didn't

191

change their policies we were going to put up posters all over town that told the public about JJ workers working sick. Then we did.

On March 22nd, 2011 Jimmy John's cleared house. They fired six of our key organizers in one fell swoop. David, Davis, Max, Forman, Micah, and myself. Besides Ayo, we were the six union members who had been involved in the campaign the longest.

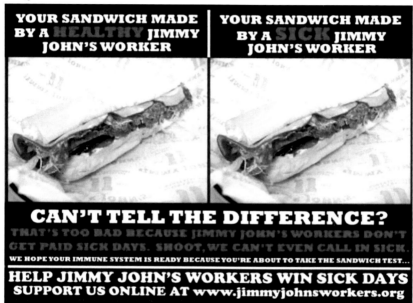

The company's argument was that we had put up posters that were disloyal to the company and disparaged the product, both unprotected activities. Nevermind that Micah was in Germany at the time and Forman was in Ohio. And most of the workers who put up posters did not get fired. Just those of us they'd identified as union leaders.

In response to the firings we did some phone zaps and marches on the boss. We came into Block E with a crowd and Forman got up in Rob's face. After that action the six of us fired workers were trespassed from the franchise's stores for one year. Our exile had begun.

We of course filed ULPs over the firings and have since then been dealing with the courts. I imagine I've made this clear by now but allow me to reiterate: Labor law is useless. Worse than useless, really, because it gives workers the illusion that they have rights.

As I write this it has been 2 years since Jimmy John's fired me. The Labor Board found merit with our ULP. They took our case to court, and the judge ruled in our favor. I still haven't been reinstated. I doubt any of us ever will. First the company appeals to the federal office of the NLRB. The Labor Board will someday rule on your case probably. The timetable is indefinite.

Then the company goes to the Court of Appeals. Again the timetable is indefinite.

Finally the company can appeal to the Supreme Court. If the Supreme Court takes the case and you're the IWW, the decision gets overturned and the union loses. Every higher court is more conservative than the last, and the Supreme Court would never side with a union devoted to the abolition of the wage system.

So, best case scenario, you were fired illegally and have a clear-cut case. Assuming you don't need money to survive and have stayed unemployed the entire time, 5 years later you will be reinstated with back pay. If you find work in the interim the company does not have to give you backpay.

The only way I know to force a company to rehire a union organizer is to strike, and I've only read about that in histories of the 1934 Teamsters Strike. At Jimmy John's we were never organized enough to strike, so all we could do was make life uncomfortable for the owners and cost them a bunch of money in legal fees.

Getting fired for organizing isn't all that bad. Beats the hell out of quitting. You get to tell off your boss *and* there's a chance that in a few years you'll get a fat check. My biggest concern is that all a future employer will have to do is Google my name to find out my union sympathies, but that's been the case since the first time I was quoted in a JJWU press release. C'est la vie. Something tells me I'll still be working till I die.

The big question is: Was it worth it? Four years, countless thousands of hours, and one knee. If I could go back to February 2007, would I try to stop myself from walking into the Dinkytown JJs and asking for a job? It's not as if we're talking about a world-changing revolutionary movement like the Arab Spring. One hospital employs many times more workers than our entire franchise. This was a union campaign for 200 fast food workers. So was it worth it?
My short answer is yes.

Since the JJWU went public Jimmy John's workers all over the country have approached us wanting to unionize. At the time I'm writing this, no campaigns in other cities have yet gone public. Maybe they never will. But I think it's fair to say our impact at Jimmy John's has spread beyond our own now-11 store franchise.
Likewise in Minneapolis our impact has been felt outside of Jimmy John's. I could speculate that we've challenged people's assumptions about the food service industry. Is there any reason these jobs can't offer workers the benefits that jobs in other industries do? Why should restaurant workers have to work sick when janitors don't? At the very least I think we proved it's possible to win a union election at a 10 store fast food franchise. Still this is all speculation.
What I know for a fact is what I've seen. And that's workers who were introduced to the IWW model of union organizing through the Jimmy John's campaign and have gone on to organize at other workplaces.
According to my organizing journal, 99 different Jimmy John's workers attended a weekly union meeting at some point

throughout the course of my involvement in the campaign[96]. Most of them are working different jobs now. I'd like to think that everyone's carried their experiences from the JJWU with them.

Then there were the Solidarity Committee members, the supporters who participated in our pickets, the customers who put those tip jars on the counters. I hope our message of direct action and solidarity had an impact on them too.

As for the friends I worked with on the committee, I believe that the JJWU had a universally empowering impact on all of them.

I remember that moment when Joe Blackseer spoke up in our meeting with the district managers over Kate's firing. Margaret wearing a union pin at the Skyway store after we lost the election even though she knew she was going to get shit for it. Wil excited when he finally got the hang of 1-on-1s and we had our first meeting with the Calhoun workers. Emily speaking at the Eyes on the Fries event. Max saving my job and making Mike J. put me back on the schedule. Andy standing outside the store in his apron with his arms crossed during the Calhoun work stoppage. All of it.

I also remember that intense sense of solidarity in the meeting after we lost the election. Me saying that I blamed myself, and everyone telling me it wasn't my fault and wanting to help me. I feel like if I had needed a ride to Tennessee and $10,000 they would have found a way. And the same went for everybody else. We were there for each other.

As for myself, I came away from Jimmy John's a very different person then I was the day I began.

When I walk into any store now I can immediately identify who's management. When a friend tells me they had a bad day at work I instinctively ask questions until we get to the root of the issue and then I try to work with them on

---

[96] I was pretty thorough in my documentation but I admit I may have missed a few. This is not counting shop committee and specific action meetings.

finding a collective solution. When I'm at a party and somebody's going on about how much they love their job I get into messy drunken arguments and tell them they're being a tool[97].

I never imagined I'd be any good at organizing. I grew up socially awkward and mentally unstable. I had poor posture and was never popular. When I started doing 1-on-1s and realized that I could connect on a very human level with all these vastly different people it was like I became a new person. I can find the good in anyone now. It's hard to put a price on that[98].

*

These days the JJWU is alive and well, but I'm not too much a part of it. I don't even know who all is on the current Minneapolis committee. I've turned down every invitation to mentor younger organizers. I see JJ workers around town and don't try to agitate them or discuss the union. My days as a fearless union organizer are past me.

As much as I was burnt out on Jimmy John's and the IWW, it's been hard being boring. Feels like something is missing. For a long time the JJWU was what gave me purpose in life. I felt like I was contributing to something larger than myself, something that made the world a better place. Now all I have is backgammon and beer. Both of which I enjoy, but neither of which satisfy me.

Writing this narrative has felt productive, but in a couple paragraphs I'll be done and I'll have to find something else to do. Where I go from here I have no idea. What I do know is that the experiences I've written about here are a large part of the person I am today. I'll never be able to unlearn what I've learned. Wherever there's capitalist enterprise I'm going to see exploitation, and I'll never be content unless I'm doing something to combat it.

---

[97] That last one doesn't usually go over too well, actually...
[98] My posture still sucks.

196

I'd like to close with my thoughts on 4-letter words. Words like fuck and shit. Probly and spose[99]. I use these words in my writing. I'm aware that they're not proper English, but I never intended this story for an academic audience.

This story is for people who speak in those 4-letter words. It's for punks who work in kitchens. It's for young activists in the Occupy movement. It's for anyone who has ever had to work a double because their night shift replacement didn't show up and there was just nobody else.

Really it's for anybody who thinks they might have it in them to accomplish what we could not. I spent 4 years of my life trying to win union recognition at an American fast food franchise with 200 workers. We lost a union election by two votes. I dare you to do better. Fucker.

*

---

[99] Yeah I know.

Thank you so much:

Aaron Kocher * Abby * Abe Coleman * Adam McNeil * Adam Smith * Alex Card * Alyssa * Andy Cullen * Angel Gardner * Anja Witek * April Glynn * Arella Vargas * Arik Xist * Arthur Daniels * Ashley Kreidler * Ayo Collins * Bart * Ben Yela * Bob Adams * Bob Hollister * Bob Kolstead * Brandon Clements * Brendan Rogers * Breon * Bri Hennesy * Brittany Koppy * Callie Bensel * Candice * Casey Setzer * Carrie Feldman * Christina Vana * Crystal Tremor * Courtney Alexander * Cyrus * Dan Rude * Dan Van Laeger * Dan Gross * Davis Ritsema * Deeg * Derek Loftis * Devo * Dirty Pete * Dezi * DJ McIntee * Dustin Dzuck * Eli Meyerhoff * Emily Barnes* Emily Pryzblski * Tall Emily * Winona Emily * Eric Andersen * Eric Corchoran * Eric Ziebart * Erica Johnson * Riverside Erica * Erik Davis * Erik Forman * Erin Stalnacher * Evan Giannoble * Evan Wolfsen * Florence * Forehead * Gaby Gagnon * Grant Richardson * Greg Rick * Hallie Wallace * Hardy Coleman * Hodan Abdi * Jaim'ee Bolte * Jake Bell * Jake Foucault * Jake Lindgren * Skyway Jake * Jane * Jared Ingebretzen * Jason Evans * Jay Krpan * Jeff Jones * Jeff Pilacinski * Jen Arbelius * Jesse Soderstrom * Jim Feldman * JJ Mangen * Jody Chandler * Joe Blackshear * Joe Smith * Joey Smiles * Joel Schwartz * Johnny Fuckcakes * Jonathon Kennedy * Joram Livengood * Jordan Lund * Julia Hatlestad * Kait Sergenian * Katie Lien * Kristi * Krystal Hoppe * Karina * Kate Cina * Kieran Knudsen * Laila Davis * Leo Garza * Lita Beach * Luc Parker * Madelene Jones * Manuel Levins-Holden * Matt Bongers * Matthias Sturn * Max Specktor * Micah Buckley-Farlee * Mike Freeman * Mojo * Molly * Nate Holdren * Neal Linder * Nick Hammer * Niko Waryan * Nitali * Noah * Parsons * Paulmer Johnson * Pammy * Pat Brenner * Paula Mayberry * Raphi * Reuben Yebra * Ricki Olsen * Robby Forever * Rorie * Rye * Sam Dungan * Sam Johnson * Sara Glesne * Savannah Reich * Scott DeMeuth * Sean Eddins * Skorpiain * Spencer Verden * Stephen Gresling * Tim Louris * Tim Roach * TJ * Todd * Tiana * Tony Jeff * Travis Erickson * Travis Minnik * SA Ty * Uriah * Von G. * Wes * Wil Olsen * Zach B. * ...and Lucius the dog.